FILMING the UNDEAD

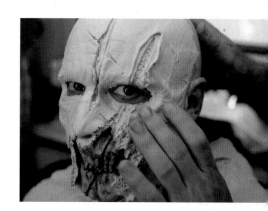

FILMING the UNDEAD

HOW TO MAKE YOUR OWN ZOMBIE MOVIE

Rod Durick

BARRON'S

First edition for the United States, its territories
and dependencies, and Canada published in 2011
by Barron's Educational Series, Inc.

Copyright © Ivy Press Limited 2011

This book was conceived,
designed, and produced by
Ivy Press
210 High Street
Lewes
East Sussex BN7 2NS
United Kingdom
www.ivy-group.co.uk.

All inquiries should be addressed to:
Barron's Educational Series, Inc.
250 Wireless Boulevard
Hauppauge, NY 11788
www.barronseduc.com

ISBN: 978-0-7641-4716-6

Library of Congress Control Number: 2011922074

Creative Director **Peter Bridgewater**
Publisher **Jason Hook**
Editorial Director **Tom Kitch**
Senior Designer **James Lawrence**
Designer **Glyn Bridgewater**
Illustrators **Rob Brandt and Kyle Kaczmarczyk**
Commissioned photography **Michelle Zurowski**

Printed in China

Color origination by Ivy Press Reprographics

9 8 7 6 5 4 3 2 1

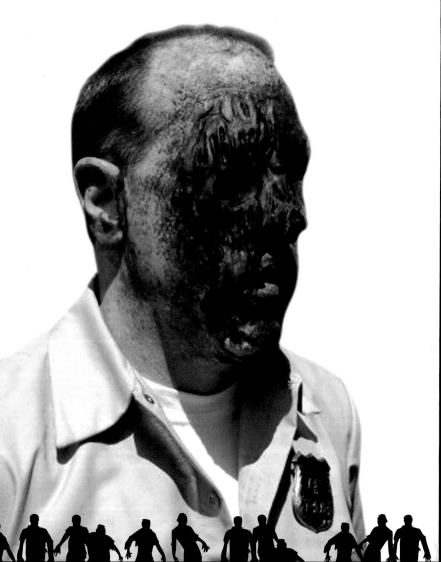

Contents

introduction

There's something about the undead—a horde of flesh-hungry, mindless beasts without a shred of decency or human emotion, swarming over a small group of would-be survivors—that makes our hearts beat faster. From the origins of the early pop-culture zombie in Haiti, to the 1932 movie *White Zombie* starring Bela Lugosi, to the George Romero franchise and all of the movies, books, and comics in between, there's something about zombies and carnage that just makes us happy.

It could be some primal fear in our collective subconscious that triggers our love for the living dead. It could be the idea that our mothers, fathers, sons, or daughters could fall prey to the undead and become zombies themselves, which forces the question of whether or not you should kill your own flesh and blood, before they kill you first. Maybe it's just that a heartless killing machine who wants nothing more than to eat us while we are still kicking is a damnable terrifying idea.

Zombie movies are a perfect outlet for these fears. Sitting in a dark theater, safe with a few of your closest friends, you get to watch all of those things from the shadowy recesses of your mind come to life.

You may be asking, "So who would want to make a zombie movie anyway?" I know my parents always thought there was something wrong with me. When other kids were clamoring to see the latest cartoon or newest feel-good family comedy, I wanted to see *Night of the Living Dead* one more time.

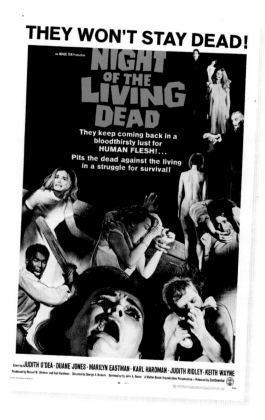

01 / Romero invented the modern zombie movie with not much more than a group of friends and an old film camera.

02 / *Shaun of the Dead* (2004) is an excellent example of the classic Romero-style zombie movie, but it was also hilarious. Comedy and horror juxtaposed can be used to great effect, but it is harder to make people laugh than it is to scare them.

I knew zombies would play a part in my future, and fortunately it wasn't because of the zombie apocalypse. It would be twenty years before I realized that I could make my own movies. I wanted to be a filmmaker. I wanted to make horror movies—zombie movies!

■ Who Is This Book For?

If you're still reading, I'm assuming you want to make movies too. So the simple answer to the question, "Who would want to make a zombie movie?" is "Us!"

You and I are zombie movie fans with the desire to put our own spin on the genre. We want to add our own little piece to the mythology of the living dead. It falls to us to put a new shine on an old and well-worn but loved pair of shoes.

Unfortunately, not all of us have connections to the Hollywood machine. Making movies for us will, most likely, be very different from what we see on all of those slick studio DVD extras. We don't have

access to millions, sometimes not even thousands, of dollars. No-budget filmmakers cannot afford to film for thirty days straight—we film when everyone we need for the scene can get time off from their day jobs. We can't afford proper catering—we eat burgers or hot dogs that the director's significant other brought from home.

The good news: We can make a good zombie movie for almost nothing if we have a group of dedicated friends, access to a camera, and a good story. So read on, brave filmmaker. We can do this.

03 / *White Zombie* (1932) is one of the greatest examples of the Haitian zombie movie. It is also the inspiration for one of the best metal bands to come out of the late nineties.

story

The first thing you need, before anything else, is a good story. Your story is more important than the actors, more important than the makeup, and more important than having many thousands of dollars worth of professional equipment at your disposal. A good idea and a strong script based on that idea will be the foundation on which you build your movie.

Some people say that there are no new story ideas left, and that everything has already been done. To a certain degree, this is true—just look at all of the remakes and sequels that are made. But this doesn't mean we can't come up with something new. How many times have you been watching a movie and thought you could make something better? Now is your chance.

Your story does not need dozens of characters, thousands of extras, or exotic locations. What it does need is a couple of characters your audience will grow to care about and maybe a character or two that your audience will grow to hate and you need to put them all in harm's way. "Harm," in this case, means a lot of zombies.

■ Storytelling Basics

At its most basic level, a story consists of just three parts—a beginning, a middle, and an end. You should also be aware of dramatic elements such as *exposition*, *foreshadowing*, *rising action*, *climax*, and *resolution*.

Beginning The beginning of the story should introduce the characters, introduce the world in which they live, and establish the overall feel of your tale. This is where you will set the groundwork for the conflicts and events to come.

Take *Night of the Living Dead* as an example. The beginning is where we meet the characters, who are trapped in the farmhouse. We learn about the types of people they are and their motivations. We get the first glimpses of the undead, *foreshadowing* things to come.

Middle The middle of the story is when the characters are thrown into a situation or presented with some obstacles that need to be overcome. This is often the part of the story where there should be some kind of *exposition*, explaining the events that have transpired, and when conflicts develop between the protagonists and antagonists (*rising action*), as the story progresses headlong toward some type of *climax*.

Continuing with *Night of the Living Dead*, the middle is when the conflict develops between Ben and Harry Cooper. Ben takes charge of the situation and adopts the role of hero; Tom and Judy choose to side with Ben, and Barbara starts to come out of her state of shock. They get some semblance of an explanation of the events from the television newsmen and they notice more and more zombies gathering outside.

End The end of the story is when the *climax* unfolds and the characters have to deal with the events that have transpired. This is when the details are wrapped up and everything that has happened over the course of the story reaches its *resolution*, be it a happy ending or not.

The ending of *Night of the Living Dead* is when they try—unsuccessfully—to reach the gas pump, when Karen Cooper gets up with a garden trowel and kills her mother, and when the zombies finally get into the house. The story wraps up when the townsfolk kill Ben.

There it is: a beginning, a middle, and an end. With these basics in mind, you can now concentrate on developing your own story.

Note

Herschell Gordon Lewis, the "Godfather of Gore," gave me the best piece of film-making advice I've ever received. He said that no one has ever walked out of a movie because of a little camera wiggle. What he meant was this: If the story is good and your characters are strong, the viewer will forgive many of your technical missteps.

01 / No matter where you are in the story, once the zombies show up, you know it is going to be good. Or bad.

research

Step number one to developing your own story: do your research. I do not mean spending hours in a library, pouring over dusty old tomes of Haitian lore; I mean that you should go watch a handful of zombie movies. Try to watch a few from each sub-genre, which is a difficult task on its own. A little bit of reading won't hurt, either.

There are many, many kinds of zombie movies. Voodoo was the culprit in *Serpent and the Rainbow* and *I Walked with a Zombie*. Medical experimentation has spawned zombies, as seen in *Resident Evil, 28 Days Later,* and *Re-Animator*. Aliens have had a hand in it with movies such as *Plan 9 from Outer Space* and *Night of the Creeps*. Radiation, sound waves, evil from the depths of hell, and even Nazis have all been the basis of zombie movies.

Try watching some non-zombie movies too, to see whether you can create a cross-genre movie.

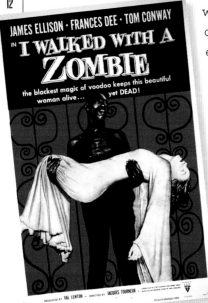

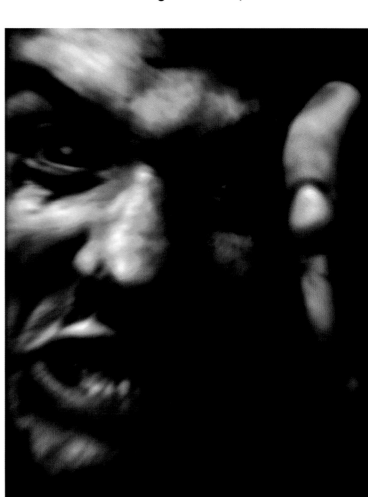

01 / Val Lewton's *I Walked with a Zombie* (1943) combined voodoo with medicine.

Science and Medicine

Medical breakthroughs and advancements in technology can always be mined for ways they could be responsible for the next zombie outbreak. Look at all the vaccines, meant to stave off the next flu pandemic, that get rushed to market. Look at the rash of medicines that have been pulled off the market because of unintended side effects, or the side effects from some of the drugs that are still on the market.

Nanotechnology is well on its way from being science fiction to science fact; robotic limbs and organ replacements have been a reality for years. Science can be terrifying. Imagine a zombie with robot arms and a titanium plate in its head protecting its brain!

02 / *28 Days Later* (2002): Fast zombies driven by medically designed unfocused rage. Fast zombies. Unfocused rage. Yeah, everyone is pretty screwed.

Two of the biggest zombie movies of recent years have been comedies: *Shaun of the Dead* and *Zombieland* (which you could also call a buddy movie). What about a zombie western, or a zombie costume drama? Think about your potential cast's singing prowess, however, before you plan *Zombie: The Musical*.

■ Zombie Brainstorming

There are hundreds of books, short stories, comics, and graphic novels dealing with the undead. Don't directly adapt a story you've read—there are all kinds of copyright issues and licensing hoops that you would have to jump through—but look at what others have done, and try to find something they missed. Try to find a path to the undead that no one has yet taken. Combine ideas into something new, simplifying a complicated idea, or even come up with an idea based on what audiences haven't seen.

Talk to your friends. The saying "more heads are better than one" is very often a true saying. Invite a group of friends over to watch some movies and talk about which scenes they think are the best. Ask them what they would like to see in a zombie movie. My friends and I have come up with some of our best ideas while sitting around the television. I'll start the exchange with something like: "You know what would be awesome? If that guy got a limb chopped off in a revolving door!" And the barrel will just start rolling from there. We have sketched out entire sequences while barely paying attention to the movie playing in front of us.

outline

Once you have a rough idea of your story, start writing things down. To sound like your high school creative writing teacher, create an outline. An outline is not always a necessary step, but it can help you to assemble a narrative structure, which will assist you when it's time to write your script.

Before you put together an outline, write down the central idea, concept, or pivotal scene that you know needs to be in the movie. Now, you need to support that idea or scene by figuring out what leads up to it and then follows from it.

Is the intrepid hero stuck in a porta-potty with hundreds of gore-soaked zombies clawing at the thin plastic walls? What is his name? Where did he come from? How did he find himself in an outhouse? Where is the outhouse? Where is everybody else? How is he going to get out?

In writing these plot points down, more things will come to you, and soon your story will begin to take on a life of its own. The more you write, the faster these ideas will come. You'll find that you have a dozen characters, each with his/her own personality traits and foibles. You'll have locations and ideas about the environments, and some idea about how your zombies will behave.

Once you have some characters and locations down, start putting together your outline—just start taking those random ideas and arranging them in some kind of chronological order. Don't worry if the brainstorming continues

as you write the outline … it's your story. You can add to it or remove whole sections, and no one can tell you otherwise.

One more thing that the outline will do for you is assist in writing your script. You will already have an idea of what happens and when; you just need to put some dialogue in the characters' mouths. This is the hard part, and the dialogue will probably change several times before your movie is done.

01 / The starting point for your movie can be a single key scene, image, or location that sticks in your mind. Use your outline to flesh out the details of the story.

Outhouse of the Dead

- Pickup truck blows a tire on a litter-strewn road that resembles the aftermath of a demolition derby.

    - Pickup hits another car.

    - Hero is thrown free because he was riding in the bed, survives.

        - Loses gun.

    - Another man riding in the bed gets thrown into a wall, doesn't survive (he comes back as a zombie later).

    - Woman riding in the bed gets thrown through a storefront window, survives.

    - Driver and Passenger both survive and enter storefront through the new hole in the window.

        - Zombies converge at the hole in the window.

        - Hero tries unsuccessfully to recover gun.

    - Hero is cut off from the rest of the group, zombies bearing down from every direction.

- Porta-potty is in easy reach.

- Hero makes for the porta-potty.

script

There are countless film school classes, books, and tutorials on how to write a script, and as many differing opinions on the correct way to write one. At the microbudget level, the format of your script is not as important as the information contained therein. The information you need to include is the dialogue, a description of the action, and a description of the location and environment.

Before you start, I would strongly suggest getting a scriptwriting software application. These are programs that will do all of the script formatting for you; some are free, others expensive.

Most of the scriptwriting applications will help you write your script, create outlines and schedules, and even number your scenes. Although not entirely necessary for a no-budget movie, a consistently formatted script will make life a lot easier, make it easier to read, and be better able to describe the setting and action.

The big-boy applications include Final Draft (www.finaldraft.com) and Movie Magic Screenwriter (www.screenplay.com)—both of these programs are very good, though they cost in excess of one hundred and fifty dollars. However, you may find a cheaper or free scriptwriting application with most or all the features you will need. I prefer to use a program called Celtx (www.celtx.com) because of its ease of use and low price point. You can download the program, install it, and be writing a script within ten minutes. Celtx will format your script, allow

Location   Action

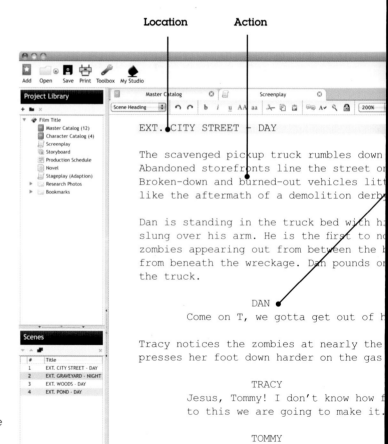

you to create a storyboard using drag and drop "clip art"-type elements, and will number your scenes to help you create your schedule.

■ Scriptwriting Tips

Know your limits Be realistic. If you don't have access to a World War II-era Sherman tank, don't write one into your story. If you don't have an accomplished actor in your group of friends, don't write a scene that will depend solely on the strength of an actor's performance.

Dialogue

reet.
ide.
reet

and
of

and

Show it, don't tell it The viewer has no idea that the zombies are drawn by the smell of blood. However, if they can see the zombies sniffing at the air and then turning toward the fresh blood, they will be able to figure it out.

Read aloud As you are writing, read out loud. Your script may sound fine in your head but seem clumsy or forced when you actually hear it. You might even want to ask someone else to read it to you.

01 / Celtx has a very intuitive interface. The enter key will cycle through the script elements–it sometime seems like Celtx knows what you need next.

Alternatively, you may have an actor in mind when creating a role and writing the dialogue. Write to that person's voice, and you'll find that the dialogue should flow easier. When that person actually reads the lines, it should sound natural.

Take a break Once your script is done, put it down for a while and try not to think about it. After a few days, pick it up and read it aloud to someone else. Something is bound to jump out at you that will require some editing.

Be flexible Don't be afraid to let the actors ad-lib some of the lines. The script is a road map. It tells you how to get from point A to point B in the story, but your actors may find a better route to the final destination.

02 / You need to be realistic with what you'll have at your disposal. Danny Boyle could wreck a London bus in *28 Days Later*; you can't in your movie.

storyboards

The tale you are trying to tell should come through in your script. But sometimes the little nuances you saw in your mind's eye may not have made the trip from your brain to the page. That's where storyboards come in. A storyboard is simply a visual reference so that everyone can see exactly how you want a shot to look.

Many microbudget movies do not have room in the budget to employ an artist to draw all of the shots in the movie. If you don't have the time or resources to storyboard your whole movie, don't worry. However, you should at least "sketch" something out for the more complex scenes.

This is especially true if there are any scenes that are integral to the story or need to be filmed exactly how they play out in your head or the movie won't work. For the important shots, you really should have something tangible as reference for your crew.

"But, I'm not an artist," you say.

"But, I don't know how to draw," you say.

Well, like everything else you do when there is no budget, you have to improvise. Even the most inept, all-thumbs toddler can scrawl out a stick figure. Stick figures and simple line drawings are more than sufficient to get your idea across.

This panel of the storyboard shows the production team that the director wants to shoot this scene from the rooftop.

01 / It turned out that filming on a construction site raised too many safety problems. We filmed the outhouse in a park, which worked with a bit of creative editing.

These two panels show the production team that the director wants the camera to track the actor as he flies from the truck.

This panel shows the production team the framing he wants when they shoot Tracy recovering from the accident before Tom.

Crude stick figures visually describing the shots are better than your assistant director filming what you don't want because he or she didn't understand what you meant in the script.

Sometimes, in the process of storyboarding, you may find that a particular scene doesn't work for some reason. This will enable you to figure out a much better set of angles and camera moves, or you might rewrite or even delete a scene completely. You would have stumbled onto this anyway if you had actually tried to shoot the scene without storyboarding, but you will save a great deal of time and money by creating some kind of storyboard first.

So, do you need storyboards? Not necessarily. Can you make your movie without storyboards?

02 / The script called for a shotgun, but at the microbudget level you need to take what you can get. In this case, we upgraded to an assault weapon.

Yes. But are storyboards useful? Absolutely! However, don't forget that the first thing you need is a good story. Once you have the story down, a script, and maybe a storyboard or two in your hands, you are ready to start the fun part.

EXT. CITY STREET - DAY

The scavenged pickup truck rumbles down a cit...
Abandoned storefronts line the street on either side. Broken down and bur...
aftermath of a demolition derby.
Dan is standing in the truck bed with his shotgun slung over his arm. He is the f...
between the buildings and from beneath the wreckage. Dan poun...

DAN
Come on T, we gotta get out of here...
Tracy notices the zombies at nearly the same time and presses her foot a...

TRACY
Jesus, Tommy! I don't know how far in to this we are...

TOMMY
Just drive baby, get us the hell out of here...
The truck quickly speeds up...Tracy swerves dangerously between the mangled...
Without warning, the truc...a tire by hitting a sharp twisted ...
into one of the wrecked ca...is thrown from the bed int...
...is thrown from the ...d into...
...sounds...
...we have to g...
...lets go...
Tom grabs his rifle form the ...of the truck a...
...around the ...the storefron...
quickly check...helps Tracy th...

preproduction

Remember when I said that you were ready for the fun part? I lied. Put simply, preproduction is getting everything ready before you start filming, and it's a grueling, life-draining, complicated, and maddening process. However, the further you get into it, the more exciting the process will become—and you'll begin to see your movie taking shape. It will start to become real.

01 / DV cameras tend to be smaller, easier to operate, and much less obtrusive than film cameras.

Digital Video or Film?

Digital video (DV) cameras have brought moviemaking out of Hollywood and into the hands of people like us. Digital video cameras are relatively affordable, and digital media is cheap. With digital, you can edit your footage on just about any computer. With digital, you can literally have the day's footage edited before you get back to the set the next morning. On the other hand, film stock is expensive, and lab fees are ludicrously high. Film is difficult to edit, and access to film-editing equipment can be very costly. So, at the microbudget level, there really is no choice.

There are a million things that you need to do before you can even think about rolling cameras. First, you need to think about a crew, contracts, permits, budgets and money, locations, and casting. I'll cover each of these topics, and a few more, in this chapter.

There is, however, a school of thought that says, "To hell with preproduction, I am just going to grab my camera and shoot this bad boy." At the no-budget level, it seems like this wouldn't be such a horrible idea. But ...

This person may have some footage at the end of the day, but it will look like he or she just grabbed a camera and filmed—the footage will look rushed, unorganized, and unprofessional. The lighting will be bad and the sound will be erratic. By failing to get permission to shoot at the location, he or she runs the risk of being arrested. There is the risk that friends cannot act to save their lives. There is the risk that when filming is wrapped and they are finished with post-

production, a feud will break out between members of the production team and an actor, and then that actor will demand his or her name be pulled from all of the marketing and promotional materials while the producers are in the middle of promoting the film to distributors.

All of this and more can be avoided by doing at least a little preproduction. You may hate every minute of it, but preproduction is a necessary evil. Take your time. If you have never made a movie before, a lot of these tasks will seem impossible. They aren't. They just require some hard work and dedication to the cause.

02 / The director wanted a scene with the actor on a chimney stack. During preproduction, they scouted a building with a 2 storey chimney.

03 / The production team took their investor kit to this town's council. They convinced the town to shut down an entire street for a full day. This would not have been possible without being diligent in preproduction

Fund-Raising

Even for a low-budget zombie movie, the first stage of preproduction is raising some money, because making your undead horde actually look like an undead horde will cost a few pennies. Do some homework before you start asking for money—break down the script to come up with a budget, and make some decisions about the look and feel of the movie.

■ Calculating Costs

As we've seen, choosing whether to shoot on film or digitally has a great effect on your budget, both at the production stage and also at postproduction. At our level of filmmaking, shooting digitally rather than on film is a no-brainer (see page 22). Once you've got that

decision out of the way, you'll have to go through the script, line by line, and look for all of the properties (props) you'll need to acquire. You have to figure out how many costumes you'll need and account for the makeup used on every zombie. You have to buy blank DV tapes or some other storage medium, depending on the camera

01 / *Evil Dead* (1981) was made largely on the back of investments from local professionals. Ask your doctor or dentist if they've ever dreamed of producing a movie.

CASE STUDY: **PETRIFIED**

Director/Producer Charles Band found a creative way to raise money to get his movie made. I have an executive producer credit on his Full Moon movie Petrified, but all I did was buy two hundred dollars' worth of Full Moon merchandise. There are a few hundred other executive producers on the movie. Think about that: Say there were two hundred "executive producers," and they all put in two hundred dollars—simple math tells us that adds up to forty thousand dollars. I am pretty sure that I can make a couple of movies with forty thousand dollars.

Investor Kit

Before pitching your idea to an investor, I'd recommend you make an "investor kit." Include a brief synopsis of the movie, describe all of the characters, and include some concept art and a storyboard or two. Detail some information about all of the film festivals you plan to submit to and how you plan to distribute and sell the movie. With this kit, you will have something tangible that an investor can hold in his or her hands. It is something for you to refer to when you are making your spiel. It might even help you to look like a real filmmaker.

you will use. You have to feed the cast and crew. You'll have to put gas in your car to get to the set. Chances are you'll also be buying a lot of coffee.

■ Finding Investors

You can fund the project yourself or ask family and friends to invest. Lately, I have seen a lot of independent filmmakers using Internet sites such as Kickstarter.com or IndieGoGo.com, where you can post a proposal and ask for donations to get your project made. These sites often entail offering "perks" to entice people to donate money—things such as free DVDs, posters, screen credits, or special thanks. I have even seen someone selling "producer" screen credits on eBay. Basically, a producer is someone who can get you what you need to get your movie made, or someone who ponies up a wad of cash to get the process going.

Always be honest with investors. It is very likely that the movie will not make any money, and they will lose their investment. Don't make them promises that will keep you on the hook to repay money they put into the project.

■ Managing Your Capital

Once you do get money to make your movie, keep it separate from your personal finances. Open a new bank account and get a debit card—this will provide you with nearly instant access to your money as well as access to online statements to see exactly how your budget stands at every point of production.

Keep every receipt. This is key to reconciling your expenditures with the bank statements. You can also line items on a spreadsheet.

Another thing about receipts—keep them for tax time. Nearly every penny you spend can be written off on your taxes. If you do wind up making money on your movie, you need to offset the gains with some losses so you don't lose everything when "the man" comes to take his share.

Legal Issues

For a no-budget or very small-budget project, you will probably not have the money to employ a lawyer. If it is at all possible, however, I suggest that you at least talk to one. Making a movie is filled with all kinds of legal pitfalls—many of which you may not even be aware of—that a lawyer can help you to avoid.

■ Contracts

It's best to have a lawyer draw up your contracts, but if you can't afford one, check in at local colleges and universities. There is bound to be a law student or a paralegal in training who would be inclined to help you put together a document that holds more weight than if you just scrawled an agreement on a bar napkin. They may even be willing to do it for screen credit and a pizza.

As a last resort, you should be able to find some sample contracts online. Take a look at them and try to write your own. In New York State, for example, contracts are legally binding as long as all parties involved sign on the dotted line. You should, however, check with your local film commission (if you have one) and do a bit of research to see if anything in particular is called for in the local statutes that you need to be aware of. Do try to get your contracts checked by a lawyer—if they're not watertight, you may be in for trouble further down the line. If your movie does manage to make money, you will be surprised at all the people who will come with their hands out looking for a slice of the pie.

Who Needs a Contract?

The simple answer is: everyone. Even if you are making a movie with your brother or your best friend, make them sign a contract. Every single person on the crew and in the cast needs to sign something. The contracts need to outline exactly what everyone in your crew will be doing, what they cannot do, and how much money, if any, they will get if the movie ever makes a profit.

You also need to get signed documents for every location you use. Even if your grandmother gives you permission to film a scene in her backyard, make sure she signs a document that says exactly that.

Make sure that you get all your actors—even the extras—to sign contracts stating that you will be allowed to use their names, voices, and likenesses in any production materials and/or derivative works until the end of time. If you have signed documents, you will avoid problems later on.

■ Insurance

Another thing you need to think about is insurance. Insurance, in most cases, is required to get a film permit. Often, you will need insurance and permits to be allowed to film at a location. We'll talk more about permits in the section about locations later in the book (see page 38).

Insurance also provides peace of mind. If someone gets hurt on your set, or property is damaged in the process of making your movie, a general liability insurance policy will cover these and protect you from personal liability.

Again, call your local film commission and ask what level of liability coverage is required to obtain a film permit and then shop around. For a permit in the Buffalo-Niagara region, for example, you need a minimum of one million dollars of liability coverage. We were able to secure a million-dollar general liability policy for six hundred dollars. This insurance covered twelve nonconsecutive days, or "slate days." A "slate day" is just that: twenty-four hours of filming. If one of your days happens to be January 12, then you are covered from 12:00:00 A.M. to 11:59:59 P.M. on January 12. At 12:00:00 A.M. on January 13, you are no longer covered. Generally, the only things the insurance company needs to know are the exact days you intend to film and if you plan to have any stunts, explosions, or anything else that would put cast, crew, or location at added physical or financial risk, but do check first.

If any insurance provider tells you that they can cover you for only consecutive days, thank them and inform them that you will be taking your business elsewhere. It is just easier for them to handle the paperwork for consecutive days.

01 / If you know your actors or crew will ever be in a position where they might get injured, insurance will be the thing that will let you sleep the night before.

crew

Now, you'll need to employ your crew. I use "employ" in the sense that you probably won't be paying anyone, so your family and friends are the first people you'll go to in order to find a team of fledgling filmmakers. If you have money for a crew, by all means, employ one with experience—but be prepared to take what you can get.

You can make a movie all on your own, but I wouldn't recommend it. You will never be able to run the camera and make sure your actors are hitting all of their marks. If you are directing, you won't have time to do any effects. If you are doing effects, you don't want to pick up the camera because you will probably have goo all over your hands. If you are planning to direct the story you've conceived and the screenplay you've written, you'll need a crew to help turn your ideas into film. The crew members you should consider using are as follows:

Producer The producer is responsible for balancing the logistical and creative sides of the movie. On a small-budget movie the producer will be doing a whole lot more, from managing the cast and crew to marketing and distribution.

Production Designer Art direction, production design … whatever you want to call the position, someone needs to handle it to give the movie a cohesive style. This person should work closely with the director, the effects team, and the

01 / Giving the director a megaphone guarantees that he will use it every second that he is on set and probably on the ride home as well.

wardrobe person to come up with the way your movie will look. If you have to build or dress any sets, the production designer is the one who will be responsible for getting it done.

Director of Photography If you plan to direct the movie yourself, you will need a director of photography (DP or DoP). While you are making

sure that your actors are nailing their lines, your DP will make sure that the shot stays in focus. A good DP will typically have his or her own camera, or be familiar with yours, and should know how to light a scene and frame shots to the best advantage.

Wardrobe Someone comfortable with combing thrift stores is a good choice to keep track of wardrobe and costuming. This person will need to make sure that the blood splatters are in the same place every day, that things get washed if you cannot film in script order, and that they can handle a needle and thread if an actor's pants require any emergency repairs.

Makeup Getting your zombies and victims into makeup is time-consuming, and the makeup artist will be concentrating on this while the director is getting the dialogue scenes shot. (See Makeup & Prosthetics on pages 70–71 for more on the subject.)

Casting You will probably not have time during preproduction to track down a bunch of actors willing to work for free. Make someone else do it.

Assistant Director The assistant director (AD) is the director's extra pair of eyes, ears, and hands. The AD will be the one wrangling with the actors and making sure everyone not involved in the current scene is doing what they need to be

doing to prepare for the next one. While the director is managing the scenes being shot, the AD is managing the rest of the set.

Production Manager or **Line Producer**
Both basically do the same thing, managing or otherwise maintaining some kind of organization for the day-to-day aspects of making the movie. At the microbudget level, this role is essential to help keep the production on schedule and on budget. This is the person in the vanguard when you move from one location to the next and essential to good relations with the local community that's playing host to your shoot.

Continuity Someone needs to control continuity. He or she will be responsible for making sure that your movie matches from shot to shot and scene to scene, so that the cut your lead actor suffered in a fight with a zombie indoors hasn't magically

02 / Everything from the color schemes in your movie to the precisely placed garbage on the street is within the domain of the production designer.

healed when the actor is seen running down the street from the house. They will also need to update the clapboard, track the scene, and maintain a shot log. (See page 108.)

Sound Recordist If any of your friends are in bands, they are the people to ask to be sound recordists. Chances are they already have some of the equipment you'll need. (See pages 94–7 for more on sound recording.)

Armorer If you have guns in your movie (see opposite), make sure there is an armorer designated to know where they are at all times, who is carrying them, and that they are not loaded. This person should keep a list on hand

and have cast and crew "sign" the weapons in and out. Before turning the weapon over to cast or crew, they armorer should check—every time—to make sure it is not loaded. I cannot stress this point enough. Check to make sure the gun isn't loaded—even a pellet gun can cause serious, permanent injury. Once again, check the local laws. If you get arrested, I will point at you and laugh and say, "I told you so."

Also, remember what I said earlier about writing to what you have access to. If realistic-looking guns are out of the question, baseball bats and all kinds of heavy, blunt sports equipment are usually fair game.

Caterer This person will make sure there is food and beverages for the cast and crew. If you aren't paying anyone, the least you can do is provide them with a meal and keep them hydrated.

Production Assistant It is inevitable that you will have forgotten something and need to pick some items up from a grocery store. The production assistant (PA) is the perfect candidate for this job. When you need to relay information to the director from the makeup crew, this is the PA's job. If someone needs to ask the driver of the ice cream truck to turn the song off, send the PA to do it. The PA is there to do just that—assist in the production, whatever that assistance might be. Depending on the size of your movie, you may need a few runners helping out the rest of the crew.

01 / You'll find that your crew will get tighter and work better together with each project that you do.

02 / PAs will be there to support you and the rest of the crew (though not always as literally as this).

Guns

Guns are tricky. In the United States, you can go into almost any department store and buy a realistic-looking BB, pellet, or Airsoft gun. However, many other countries have much tighter controls on both real and replica guns (in the UK, replica guns are controlled as tightly as real firearms). If you are going to be doing anything with weapons, make sure you know the local laws and statutes, and definitely let local law enforcement know what you are doing. One of my colleagues was arrested for menacing with a firearm because he had a realistic-looking toy gun on the front seat next to him as he was driving down the highway. He still makes it a point to tell everyone that he is the only one of us to have gone to prison for his art.

Stills Photographer Have a photographer on hand during production. You will need some good stills for your publicity material when you come to marketing your movie.

Editor Though you will have your own ideas on how the scenes you've shot will cut together to make a movie, an editor is a very useful resource, both creatively and technically. A good editor will know the software and the best workflow, and help deliver the required effects, grading, and sound design.

For a no-budget movie, you may have to do the job of five people all by yourself, but the movie will be much easier to make if you have three or four dedicated people at your side, even if they're each taking on multiple responsibilities as well. Just make sure everyone knows what roles they are playing.

However, if you don't know anyone that can do makeup, have no one to run the camera, or don't know any actors, do not fret. You can always hit a free online classified ads site such as Craigslist.org, and sites geared toward jobs for film professionals such as ProductionHub.com are also excellent resources for finding cast and crew. Many metropolitan areas have a weekly local arts paper. For a few dollars you can place an ad in the classified section to solicit cast and crew.

But remember to be honest in your ads. If you look beyond your circle of friends and family for cast and crew, make it clear that there will more than likely be no payment for services rendered.

cast

Casting your movie, or choosing the actors to portray all of the characters, will be another challenge. If you have never been involved in making a movie before, you may not know any actors. You can cast your friends in the roles, but your friends may not be able to pull off the dialogue or deliver the action with the emotion and passion the parts require.

■ Friends & Family

This is why auditions are a good idea. You don't want to be on set, with camera rolling, only to find that you made a horrible decision in choosing a particular actor. You should already have an idea, after writing the script and developing the story, of how your characters should look and of their mannerisms and behaviors. You should know that the gruff prison guard won't be best played by your seventeen-year-old asthmatic cousin. However, at the no-budget or microbudget level, you will probably have no choice but to cast some of your friends and family. I made a suggestion back in the first

chapter that you'd often have an actor in mind, and that you should write to that person's voice. This is the exact reason I made that suggestion. You know how your friends talk; you know their phrases and how they put sentences together, as well as the cadence or rhythm to their speech. If the dialogue is written specifically for one of your friends, that friend should be able to deliver a believable performance. At the very least the delivery of the dialogue should not sound forced.

01 / Half of these extras are directly related to members of the crew, the other half drove the first half to the set and were able to be convinced that being a zombie would be fun.

■ The Community

Regardless of whether you cast your friends or not, you should put out some type of casting call. You will want some options when choosing actors, because sometimes your friends will not be the right people for the roles. As I mentioned earlier, go to online classified sites, or put an ad in the classified section of the local arts paper. You can check to see if local colleges have theater or drama departments and put flyers up there. Other great places to look for volunteers are various social networking sites such as Facebook (www.facebook.com) and MySpace (www.myspace.com). If you ask every one of your friends on Facebook to ask all of their Facebook friends if they know any actors who would like to be in a zombie movie, you are bound to get some volunteers. On our last movie, we put out a Facebook request for zombie extras. We had well over one thousand people respond and nearly as many show up to be in the movie.

When you put out the casting call, make sure you describe the movie, the characters you need, and what is in it for them. Always be clear if the role is going to require anything unusual such as nudity or extensive makeup, although even if you are not paying anything, you will be surprised at how many volunteers you'll get.

Independent Zombie Film Needs Actor

Independent Zombie Film Needs Actors
No pay, weekend shoots, meals provided on filming days. Will be provided with a copy of the film and production stills for your portfolio.
- Male, 18–35, approx 6' tall, clean shaven, athletic build a plus. Physical role—may require a lot of running and/or choreographed fighting.
- Female, 18–25, 5'5" to 5'9" tall, long hair, athletic build a plus. Physical role—may require a lot of running and/or choreographed fighting.
- Female, 25–45, any height, short hair, any build. Role may require nudity or implied nudity. Must be willing to be in effects makeup for an extended period of time.

02 / Casting calls will ensure that you have options. Also, if you ever decide to make another movie, you'll have some idea as to what kind of actors are around.

■ Auditions

Now that you have some interested potential actors, you need to schedule auditions for them. The pros will tell you not to hold auditions at your house because it looks unprofessional, but I also think there are some safety and security issues involved with bringing complete strangers into your home. If you don't choose an actor and then he or she turns out to be "unbalanced," the last thing you want is for that person to know where you live.

However, spending money on an office for a few days to hold auditions is, in my opinion, a waste of money. Check around because there is bound to be a community center or a local library nearby that will let you use one of their rooms to hold your auditions. Even if it's not free, it should still be less expensive than renting an office.

Wherever you hold the casting sessions, make sure you have something nonalcoholic to drink and restrooms readily available. Also make sure that you have a couple of people in your crew on hand, preferably representing both sexes, just in case one of the people you're casting does turn out to be a little unbalanced (filming the casting session will also help).

When the hopefuls come in, give them a release form to sign that gives you permission to film the audition and give them a section of the script. This small section of script is commonly

Note

For one of the movies on which I worked, auditions were held in the crematory building at a local cemetery. There was a large hall in the building that was not being used for any ceremonies on that day, and the director secured permission to use the facility. They even gave me a tour of the facility and showed me how the ovens worked.

referred to as a "side." It's basically just a scene or two containing some of the dialogue and maybe some description of the setting.

Give them a chance to read it and ask any questions about the character. Have another actor or the casting director read the other parts in the side so you can get an idea of how the actor will interact with other performers. Make sure you take notes on each person, detailing what you liked or didn't like about the performances.

Choose your actors carefully. Balance your decision on the quality of the performance versus how close the actor looks like what you had initially envisioned. Your choice must also depend on the availability of the actor to adhere to the schedule you have in mind. Make sure you choose a backup actor or two for each part in case your first choice has to decline later once you get your schedule set in stone, or something happens that makes it impossible for the actor to play the part. Remember, you are not paying anyone, so you will need to be flexible.

01 / Choosing actors that bring their own wardrobe and costumes is a real help for microbudget moviemaking.

Film Your Auditions

- Get the actor to give you their name and information on camera. This will make it easier for you to keep the auditions straight later.

- People read differently on screen than they do in person. You may not have liked the performance live, but you could see something shine through on the video that might change your mind.

- If you have the auditions on video, you can keep going back and rewatching as you narrow your selections down.

CASTING FORM

Name #: Dave Weston

Looks: 5' 11", about 180 pounds and pretty athletic. Cropped dark hair. Average appearance.

Voice: As rough as sandpaper—might be quite good for some roles.

Acting ability: He has some previous experience from helping out on a friend's short movie, but very limited range. Probably ok in a supporting role.

Availability: Free most weekends, but he will need a few weeks' notice to get time off work to shoot midweek.

Zombie factor: We think he'd be fine, but he'd rather be kicking zombie butt than having his butt kicked. Could probably convince him though.

Notes: Friend of Christine's. Very keen to get involved after seeing her in our last movie. Probably expects to be the star, but he seems to have a good sense of humor and so he should be ok once we've persuaded him that being bitten by a zombie and joining the undead is pretty cool as well.

02 / Make sure you take notes on each person, detailing what you liked or didn't like about their performances.

Cast

35

Locations

So far, you have a good story, a script, a few storyboards, a little bit of money (we can dream, right?), a crew, some actors, and contracts signed for everything. Now you need to figure out where you are going to film your movie. As usual with low-budget moviemaking, the first step is to ask your friends and family.

From the process of developing the story, you probably have a good idea of the types of locations you need. The first thing you have to do is take an inventory of the entire cast, crew, and whatever friends and family you have who aren't already in the movie. Ask all of them if they have access to any locations that can pass for settings appropriate to the story. The odds are pretty good that someone in the mob you have assembled will have almost exactly what you are looking for.

■ There's No Place Like Home

Try to secure locations within your circle first. If she lets you film at her house, the leading man's mother will likely be fairly tolerant of the chaos caused when making a movie. On another movie on which I worked, the director got permission from his aunt and uncle to film on their six-acre wooded property. It did not cost us a dime, and it was a great location with woods, streams, and open fields. There was even a broken down, derelict cabin near the back of the property—and we made excellent use of it.

01 / Great locations are all over the place. If you find a place that you like, ask around—someone you know may have access to it.

■ Location Scouting

If you have exhausted all of the options within your circle, then you have to go do some location scouting. "Location scouting" is just what it sounds like: you go out and scout around for a location. If you need a warehouse, drive around and look for some interesting warehouses. If you want to film in a theater, go look at a few movie houses and classic theaters. If you need to film in an office, there is bound to be someone in your crew who works in one. Find out where it is and go have a look. Abandoned buildings, parks, beaches, playgrounds, mansions, whatever you need—all of these locations are out there. You just need to go find them.

■ Insurance, Permits, and Permissions

Many locations will require that you have a film permit and insurance before they allow you to shoot there. Your local film office or film commission will tell you what is required and how to obtain a permit. This is usually to protect those responsible for the location from liability if someone gets hurt. Some property owners may allow you to film if you just ask nicely, but make sure you get written permission and include them and their property in your general liability insurance.

If you do get insurance and permits, the film office will be more inclined to help you secure locations over which they have jurisdiction, and you are more likely to persuade property managers to let you use their locations.

Once you find the perfect location, you need to get permission to use it. Just because you have a film permit does not mean you can just go and shoot wherever you like. If you don't get permission, chances are you will be arrested and/or fined for trespassing. To get permission, you have to determine who is in charge of the location and ask them directly. Abandoned buildings will often have a realtor's number posted somewhere on the property. If no contact information is posted, the film office should be able to help you track down who owns the property (assuming you have a permit). If you need to film a scene at a barber shop, go in and talk to the owner. If you want to film at a public park, talk to the head of the local parks and recreation department.

Approach it like a businessperson. Be prepared to give an entire presentation about the movie, what will be in it for the location, and why you should be allowed to film there. Bring out that investor kit I suggested you put together (see page 25), and give a copy of it to each person who has a say in whether or not you can use the location. Bring a portfolio containing samples of your work and the work of your effects artists. If possible, have a demo DVD of anything you have done prior. Be honest in what you need from the location. You can talk up your movie, but be prepared to back up the talk. And, finally, be willing to take "no" for an answer.

Make sure that whoever is in charge of a location signs a contract clearly stating that you are allowed to film there.

01 / On this day's shoot, the police showed up on the set with cuffs and Tasers at the ready. They almost seemed disappointed when they learned that we had secured permission to film here.

On one of my own film projects, we were able to shut down nearly an entire village for a full day. The village closed their main street for a half mile, including the streets that intersected it. We had permits and insurance, but more importantly the production team made a convincing argument to the town council in their own favor. We asked for only what we needed, guaranteed that there would be several hundred people from out of town walking around the village business district for the whole day, and promised that we would have completely finished and cleaned up before the start of the next business day.

02 / Ask and ye shall receive. Sometimes. This village shut down a half mile of Main Street, right through the middle of their business district.

There were other concerns regarding safety and emergency plans, but eventually permission was granted to allow us to film in the village, and they agreed to shut down Main Street. Every single business on Main Street made money that day. We brought well over four hundred extras with us to their little village. One restaurant even ran out of food, and the owner had to go shopping to keep up with the demand.

schedule

Probably the most difficult part of the preproduction process will be scheduling. You need to schedule every single detail in your movie and also be prepared for the inevitable heartbreak when nothing goes according to plan. Before making a schedule, you need to break down the script.

To break down the script, you need to read through it a few times and make notes on each pass. Sort the script out by location, by actors, by time of day, by what makeup the characters are in at the time, and by any other detail that affects where and when you should shoot.

The typical script page is about eight or so inches long, and there is a standard industry format where you break down each script page into eight one-inch sections. This will help you better organize your scenes and build a schedule because you can be much more accurate in estimating how long a scene will take to shoot—if your goal is to get six pages done in a day, you don't want your schedule telling you that a scene is two full pages long when it is really only one and one-eighth pages long. Put each scene on an individual breakdown sheet (use the template provided opposite).

Once you have the script broken down, print out all of your breakdown sheets and sort them into different piles. First, give each location its own pile. Then take each location pile and sort it into day and night piles. Now you should have two piles for each location, assuming there are scenes at both night and day. You need to further sort out the day and night piles into interior and exterior scenes and according to required actors, makeup effects, or complicated action sequences.

Figure out, realistically, how many pages you can get through in a day. A dialogue scene, with minimal camera moves and setups, will take much less time to accomplish than a scene with a lot of action and characters in makeup. You will realistically get a maximum of twelve productive hours, including meals and breaks, out of your cast and crew in a day. It may take an hour to set up a scene and get it shot. I wouldn't try to do anything more than five or six pages per day. Any more than that and you run the risk of worrying more about getting to the next scene instead of getting the scenes you need shot well.

The most mind-wracking part of this whole process is coordinating when all of the actors and required crew will be available, and if cast and crew availability meshes with when you can use a particular location. Be prepared to negotiate (or beg) to get everyone on the same page.

SCRIPT BREAKDOWN

Scene #: 47		
Location: 4 / 8	Scene Description: Dan runs through the alley.	

	INT	EXT	DAY	NIGHT	Breakdown Page #: 51
					Page Count: 4 / 8

Cast: Dan—1, Tom—5, Tracy—6, Amanda—7, Walt—8

Extras: 10 Hero Zombies, 4 Construction Worker Bodies, 3 Pedestrian Bodies

Background Extras: 25 Background Zombies

Makeup Effects: 10 Hero Zombies, 25 Background Zombies, 7 Chewed-on Bodies, Cut on Tracy's head, Scratches on Tom's arm, Fresh Cut over Dan's eye

Props: Crashed Truck, Derelict Vehicles, Broken Store Window, Body Stumps 2 and 3, Rifle*, Shotgun*, fake garbage.

Art Direction: Blood on storefront, Grafitti on walls—"Goddamn Zombies"—Papers strewn on street, Trash can fire across from the store.

Wardrobe: Tom in jeans, white T, and fishing vest. Walt in cords and flannel shirt. Dan in jeans and gray T. Amanda in torn wedding dress. Tracy in ripped black pants and green hoodie.

Crew: Rod, Bob, Jay, Adam, Nick A., Kyle, Steph, Anomaly Crew and John, Nick M., and Janeen. Mike O on Stills.

Setups: 20, plus a lot of handheld

Notes: Same crew and extras from scenes 45 and 48. Get a lot of stills, Almost no dialogue, A lot of running, get Adam's "steadycam" rig. Ask Arick about camera setup for possible vfx for city backdrop.

* Sign out guns from Nick A.

01 / On your script breakdown sheets, number each scene consecutively and assign a number to each speaking role.

02 / Transpose the information from your breakdown sheets into a detailed schedule, as shown in the sample below.

Sched. Day	Location	Scene #	Scene Description	# of pages	Breakdown #	INT/ EXT	DAY/ NIGHT	Characters	# of Extras	Makeup Gags
3/12	City Street/Alley	47	Dan runs through the alley towards construction site	4/8	51	EXT	D	1,5,6,7,8	42	10 HZ, 25 BGZ, 7 Bodies
4/12	Construction site	48	Dan hides in Port-a-John	1 2/8	52	EXT	D	1,5	39	10 HZ, 25 BGZ, 4 Bodies, 2 Hedshts.

Read-Through

One of the things you'll need to build into your schedule is a read-through or a table read. This is when you get the whole cast and crew together to read through the script in its entirety. This will most likely be the first time all of the chosen actors and assembled crew will be in the same room together.

The purpose of the read-through is, in my opinion, threefold. First, it will give everyone a chance to introduce themselves.

Second, you'll want to hear the full dialogue delivered by the assembled cast, and discover if any actors have trouble with lines. This will be the time to alter the script. You can add or change lines so the dialogue sounds better or flows more naturally. The read-through will also probably be the first time many people experience the full script. If there is something wrong in continuity or some other problem in the structure of the story, someone is likely to spot it. You can also get more accurate timings and adjust the schedule accordingly.

Finally, the read-through is when you'll start to foster a spirit of camaraderie between the cast and the crew. You want everyone to be comfortable and the mood to be relaxed from the very beginning. If the cast is at ease and, hopefully, enjoying themselves, you'll be able to see the chemistry forming between them. This is important because you will all be spending a lot of time together in the near future.

01 / Even if you change a line in the read-through, you may find you need to change it again when you're on set.

I would strongly recommend filming the read-through. You might want to go back to it later and hear a particular line from an actor again. You may also find that during the read-through, you and the cast ad-lib a fantastic addition to the script. If you have it on video, you will find it very simple to transcribe the new dialogue into the shooting script.

■ Rehearsals

It is a good idea to rehearse complicated dialogue exchanges and to rehearse with an actor who has a long, unbroken section of dialogue. You should also rehearse any stunts or choreographed fight scenes and practice them over and over. If you do this ahead of time, the actor will know what to expect on the day and will be prepared to do it in as few takes as possible.

All of the first-tier hero zombies should be rehearsed. I have found that some people tend to naturally think zombies are stiff-legged, lurching creatures that stagger, arms outstretched, toward any living target. I call them the Frankenstein leg draggers. Whenever we get a group of extras ready to be zombies, I always make it a point to tell them, "Just because you are dead does not mean that you do not have any knees. Your balance may be a bit off, and you are probably a little stiff, but all of your joints are still there."

Finally, after the read-through, you may determine that some of the cast need extra rehearsal time. You'll want to make sure that anyone who seemed to have a bit of trouble gets a chance to rehearse their scenes. As a matter of fact, rehearsals are not a bad idea for the entire cast. Unfortunately, at the microbudget level, you may not have time to arrange them.

02 / Spend some time working with your zombie extras— you want them to be scary and realistic, not "Frankenstein leg draggers" that will make people laugh.

Makeup, special effects, and props

A zombie movie will not be much of a zombie movie if you don't have any undead wandering around gnawing on the villagers. If there is no blood smeared on the windows and doors, and no intestines draped over a clothesline, something will just seem off. This chapter covers everything you need to know about DIY gore.

A very important part of a successful zombie movie will be the makeup on the zombies. Unless you have access to a voodoo witch doctor, a pile of tetrodotoxin, a vial of that blue stuff from the Resident Evil movies, or you have figured out some other way to raise the dead, you will need some makeup. Not only will you need to make up the zombies, you'll need to make up the victims. If the survivors in the film have any bumps on the head, scratches, cuts, or bruises, the makeup artists will have to apply them. If there are blood splatters on the street or severed limbs in the gutter, your makeup people are sure to be the source of it all.

By this point, you will likely have an idea of how you think your zombies should look. Settling on a look for your zombies is nearly as important as having a good story. Some zombies may be gaunt figures, with their brow line and cheekbones almost protruding through the skin. Some zombies might be dry, mummified, dusty creatures, while the skin on some other zombies just turns an ashen blue-gray color.

You don't want to spend the entire first act setting up the drama and developing all kinds of tension just to have the audience laugh when the first zombies show up. However, if the zombies are just painted white with black raccoon eyes, chances are that is exactly what will happen.

This chapter will cover a lot of information on materials and techniques. Making prosthetic pieces, building props, and creating a few other reasonably advanced effects gags will be difficult if you're new to makeup and special effects. But rest assured: I will also cover the basics for those times when there is no time or money for advanced makeup.

01 / Good makeup stands the test of time. *Zombie* came out in 1979, and the zombie featured on the poster looks better than some of the zombies coming out of Hollywood today.

02 / Who says clowns are scary? Zombie clowns, maybe, but regular clowns—not so much. Actually, a well-done zombie clown is pretty terrifying.

safety and Hygiene

In makeup work, special effects or otherwise, safety and hygiene are of paramount importance. This section is written specifically for your new makeup crew. Even if your makeup artists have experience, make them read this and then explain to you their methods and procedures relating to safety and hygiene.

■ Allergies and Irritants

Many of the products used in the makeup industry are known allergens and irritants. It is your responsibility to find out if any of your actors know if they have any issues with the materials the effects team plans to use. Even if the actor thinks there should be no issues, an allergic reaction, skin or eye irritation, or even serious injury can occur if the proper technique is not followed or the makeup crew is unaware of behaviors that a material exhibits.

It is always a good idea to do a makeup test on your actors. A drop of liquid latex or a bit of platinum-base silicone on the inside of the elbow can tell you in a matter of minutes if there is a problem. Latex allergies are more common than you would think. The reaction to latex can be anything from a tingling sensation to hives to severe burning and blistering. Silicone sensitivity is extremely rare but not unheard of. Gelatin is a great alternative to latex and silicone, because it rarely causes any kind of skin irritation. Gelatin is, however, made from animal by-products, which may be a problem for your vegan actors.

Hygiene

Good hygiene practices are extremely important. Never use a sponge or other disposable applicator on more than one actor. If you use brushes, make sure they are sterilized between each use. Any tool that will come in contact with an actor or the makeup palette needs to be sterilized between each application. Dirty tools and brushes can easily spread eye and skin infections. Your cast won't be too happy if there's an outbreak of conjunctivitis within your community, and your makeup artist will be hard-pressed to find work again. As a filmmaker, you'll be unlikely to find actors willing to volunteer for you again.

As a general rule, I will never apply a product to an actor that I have not first tested on myself. I want to know what to expect from a material, so that I can let the actors know what to expect and not make them the guinea pigs.

■ Makeup Safety

Every company will provide you, upon request, with a material safety data sheet (MSDS) on any of the products you might use. The MSDS contains all of the pertinent information regarding a material. The components that comprise the material, known health hazards, first aid measures, the material's combustion temperature, the type of protective gear you should use while handling the material, and other similar types of information can all be found on an MSDS. You should familiarize yourself with the MSDS for all of the products in your makeup kit.

Airbrushing Some products are tested and certified as skin safe. Many liquid makeup brands have been used for decades with no problems. However, a lot of these materials were meant to be sponged or brushed on to the skin. A number of makeup brands are tinted with heavy metals or contain silicates that, when applied by hand, are perfectly safe, but when run through an airbrush, inhalation becomes a hazard. Contact the company that produces any product you hope to run through an airbrush. They should be able to tell you if there are any hazards of which you should be aware.

Another thing about airbrush makeup: You never want to airbrush an actor's face, especially near the eyes, at anything above twelve or fifteen PSI. Any pressure beyond that and you risk injuring the actor. You can use higher pressures to paint the body of an actor, but never more than thirty to forty PSI.

Plaster and cement Plasters and gypsum cements are common mold-making materials in the special effects industry. When mixed with water, plaster and cement begin what is called an exothermic chemical reaction. This is a complicated way of saying that they will get extremely hot. Cement will get hot enough to burn you. If you intend to make a mold or a cast of any part of the human body—any part—never, ever, just cover it in plaster. Always use a skin-safe mold material such as alginate to capture the detail of the subject, and then use plaster bandages as a rigid "mother mold." Learn the materials and follow all of the safety precautions outlined in the MSDS.

I have used Ultracal-30 (UC-30), a very hard and accurate powder gypsum cement, for several years without incident, because I made myself aware of the potential hazards before I used the material for the first time.

01 / Be careful when using makeup, or your actor may end up like this for real.

■ Pneumatic gags

Many effects gags require blood to splatter, pus to ooze, or veins and pustules to pulsate, so you need to be aware of pneumatic safety. Pneumatics is the most cost-effective way of accomplishing these gags. Air compressors, garden sprayers, and pumps of all kinds can be used as the motive force in pushing the blood and slime through your effects rigs. When doing these types of gags, always keep pressure in mind. Air at high pressure can be very dangerous.

Never fire a pneumatic gag directly into an actor's face unless he or she is wearing some type of eye protection. Never fire a pneumatic gag into an actor's ear unless he or she is wearing ear protection. Ear plugs are not sufficient because the pressure can force the plug deep into the ear canal. You do not want to risk blinding or deafening an actor.

Make sure you know the burst pressure of the hoses and the functional pressures of the valves that control the airflow. Exceeding these pressures can cause serious injury or death if a component of the rig were to burst while attached to the actor. Never leave a line charged with air. If you have a gag prepped, and the director needs to stop and reset, disconnect the gag from the air supply and drain the pressure.

Finally, always announce to the crew and actors when an air line is charged. A simple announcement of "line charged" will ensure that the crew steps a little more carefully around you and your pneumatic setup and that they are aware there is a gag ready to be fired.

01 / Always explain to the actors what the blood gag is going to do, and make sure they know how they are supposed to react to it.

■ Blades and Blunt Instruments

Sometimes an effect will call for a blade cut, slash, or stab. It's common sense, but dull any blades or points before using them in a scene—your audience will never be able to tell whether a blade is sharp or not. Warning: Dulled knives, swords, and machetes can still cause major injury if swung, full force, at a limb. The same thing holds true for any blunt objects. You can easily break someone's bones if you hit him or her with a baseball bat. A hockey stick to the head is likely to kill a person.

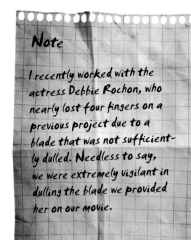

Note

I recently worked with the actress Debbie Rochon, who nearly lost four fingers on a previous project due to a blade that was not sufficiently dulled. Needless to say, we were extremely vigilant in dulling the blade we provided her on our movie.

■ Explosives and Fire

Don't use explosive squibs when pneumatic gags are just as effective and infinitely safer. In New York State, for example, you cannot legally buy squibs unless you are a licensed and insured pyrotechnician. It is potentially a crime to make explosive squibs on your own. The law tends to frown on homemade explosive devices.

The last word on safety is this: No fire. No fire at all. Fire is a hazard we cannot afford. Fire and explosives are dangerous, and you are likely to get hurt or killed. You will be arrested.

Fire—Just Say No

Don't set anyone on fire. Ever. This seems like an obvious thing to say, but I have had to refuse people who've asked if I could do it. The risk is too high. Professional stunt people train for years and have all of the requisite protective gear and equipment to pull fire gags off safely. At our level, we do not. Again, don't set anyone on fire. Ever.

02 / A baseball bat is a good zombie-killing weapon. But to be safe, we gave the actor a soft foam prop bat, just in case he got caught up in the moment.

effects breakdown

Every zombie, bruise, blood smear, and chunk of meat dangling from a radiator grill has to be accounted for in the budget. To help the director and the producers figure out the movie's total budget, the special effects makeup supervisor will need to create an effects breakdown. This involves going through the script, line by line, and flagging anything that requires a dab of makeup or a drop of blood.

You need to read through the script with a highlighter in hand. Every time you see anything that even remotely resembles an effects gag, highlight the entire section. Even something as minor as a smudge of blood on a wall needs to be noted. You should read the script through a few times, because you may easily miss something on the first pass because it may not be explicit in the script that an effect is needed. Furthermore, you may not realize how much work they will actually entail. Talk to the rest of the production team to figure out how far they want you to go with each gag.

The effects breakdown is not as standard as a script breakdown or a schedule, and it will differ with each effects person that looks at a script. For reference, this is the way I break down all of the effects scenes.

01 / The zombies that Tracy notices are the same zombies that Dan noticed, but I still make a note of it. Making sure you know exactly where each of the effects are in the script will make your job easier.

EXT. CITY STREET - DAY

The scavenged pickup truck rumbles down a city s Abandoned storefronts line the street on either Broken-down and burned-out vehicles litter the s like the aftermath of a demolition derby.

Dan is standing in the truck bed with his shotgu slung over his arm. He is the first to notice the zombies appearing out from between the buildings from beneath the wreckage. Dan pounds on the roo the truck.

           DAN
   Come on T, we gotta get out of here …

Tracy notices the zombies at nearly the same ti and presses her foot down harder on the gas ped

          TRACY
   Jesus, Tommy! I don't know how far in
   to this we are going to make it.

          TOMMY
   Just drive baby, get us the hell out of
   here. Shit they are everywhere.

The truck quickly speeds up as Tracy swerves dangerously between the totaled vehicles and o covering the road. Without warning, the truck a tire by hitting a sharp twisted chunk of met Tracy loses control and the pickup slams into of the wrecked cars. Dan is thrown from the be an overturned dumpster. The contents cushion h
from the bed into the

Page #	Scene #	Description	Materials/Technique	Need to Get - Effect	Need to Get - Fabrication	Notes
1	45-47	Drooling zombies	Silicone appliances, blood, mouth gunk	Gel-10, Naphtha, Stacolors, greasepaint, methyl and/or ultraslime, paint, pigments, flocking, frosting dye, mouthwash, toothblack	NSP clay, UC-30, alginate plaster bandage	Full face prosthetics
"	"	Bodies	Gelatin appliances, blood, blood oozing, body stumps	Gelatin kit, witch hazel, Stacolors, greasepaint, methyl and/or ultraslime, paint pigments, oxy tubing, heat shrink tube, 60cc syringes, mannequin legs and torsos, great stuff, rd-407 giblets	NSP clay, UC-30	Wound trays for extras, body stumps, and body parts
1	45	Plate window	Candy glass windowpane	Sugar, corn syrup, salt	Large pot, candy thermometer, Moldmax-20 for window mold.	

Once you are satisfied that you have marked every gag that will feature in the movie, create a new spreadsheet. You'll need to include columns for script page, scene number, a description of the gag, the technique you think will accomplish the gag, the materials you think you'll need to use, and a spot for notes. If you're not directing the movie, after you've broken the gags down you should meet with the director and explain each gag and how you see it happening. Adjust the breakdown if the director envisions a different gag or effect than what you've described.

Look at the materials columns on the finished breakdown and transfer them to another spreadsheet. Make columns for quantity/size; the name of the material; the best price you can find for the material; and the vendor, website, or local store.

Once your budget is done, meet with the director again. This time you'll need to explain the need for each material and how it is used for the gags. Now you, collectively, have to make some decisions on things to cut. You can choose to do all of the gags with gelatin and save on the cost of silicone. You can choose to have Amanda hit the ground instead of going through the window, or to make all of the prosthetic

Buying in bulk

Use your effects breakdown to work out whether you can buy some materials in large quantities to save on costs. Be sure your budget will cover the effects for the majority of a feature-length movie. You might need more gelatin or silicone here and there, but the rest of the supplies might last through to the end of production.

02 / Putting all the materials down on paper will let you see how much of each item you will need. If every gag uses silicone, you know you will be safe ordering it in bulk.

appliance pieces generic and eliminate the need for face castings. These changes alone will save hundreds of dollars.

In this chapter, I will go over a few of the most important makeup techniques using many of the materials available. I will explain the pros and cons of each material and give a brief example of how the products work. You can use this to help determine what you can afford and what your makeup crew can handle.

materials

There are many materials you can use to create effects makeup, and your choice will be based on the budget, length of time allotted to achieve each gag, and several other variables that will be unique to each production. The following pages will introduce you to several materials common to the makeup effects industry.

■ Silicone

The silicone used in the makeup industry is not the stuff the plumber uses to caulk your bathtub. Platinum-based silicone is a skin-safe material that, with a few additives, can be made to imitate the look, feel, and movement of real flesh.

Platinum-based silicone typically comes as a two-part system. Formulations differ between manufacturers, but it is typically mixed in equal parts A and B. Mixing pigments and flocking (tiny fibers that add dimension and depth to a prosthetic appliance) into one component prior to mixing them together will give a homogeneous color to the entire silicone piece. Once part A and part B are mixed together, you will have anywhere from five to ten minutes of working time, and about thirty to sixty minutes' time to demold an appliance. Silicone cures as a result of a chemical reaction, as opposed latex, which has to dry.

Silicone is expensive in relation to latex or gelatin, but knowing that almost no one will be allergic to it and the speed with which you can work makes it well worth the extra cost.

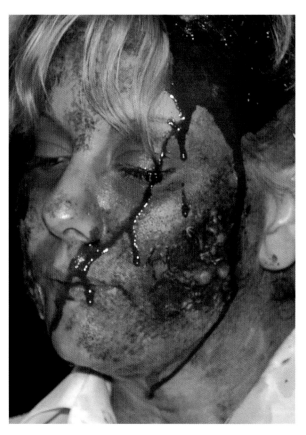

01 / The pustules on the side of this actor's face are made from skin-safe, platinum-based silicone. The piece moved and flexed as she talked (well, groaned hungrily) and stayed in place until it was removed.

Pros Silicone allergies are exceedingly rare, and the material is generally well tolerated among all skin types. Silicone has excellent flexibility and will rebound to its original shape when stretched. Silicone can be intrinsically colored (where pigments are added to a material before the material is cured) or painted. Silicone can also be used as a skin-safe adhesive. It can be thickened with inexpensive additives so that it can be applied directly to the skin and sculpted into realistic-looking wounds, and it can be brushed or poured into molds. The thickness of a silicone appliance will not affect the length of time it takes to cure.

Cons Silicone forces you to work quickly, and it's hard to extrinsically color (painting or coloring a material after it has cured). Nothing sticks to silicone but more silicone. Most pigments will rub or flake off relatively easily. Silicone will not cure in the presence of latex, and latex will not adhere to cured silicone. Therefore, it's important to clean your tools and molds if you are using both materials since silicone may not cure if latex and/or latex residue is present on them. Tin-based silicones are also available, but tin contains lead. Therefore, tin-based silicones are not skin safe. Tin-based silicones are primarily used in making molds.

02 / Liquid latex is usually a milky white color and can be as thin as cream or as thick as yogurt, depending on the vendor.

■ Latex

Many appliances are easily achieved with liquid latex; it is indispensable in making props and body parts. Liquid latex is typically a milky white color and will slowly become more translucent as it dries. Intrinsic colors may appear to be pastel until the latex is dry. Latex is easy to extrinsically color, but it is recommended that you seal an appliance with castor oil prior to adding color, because latex will absorb many colorants.

Pros Liquid latex is typically around one-fifth the cost of silicone, depending on the quantity purchased. Latex can be brushed into molds, but it should not be poured unless you are slush casting a piece (slush casting is when you pour a material into a mold, let a skin form, then pour the remaining material back into its original container).

Cons Thick layers or thick pours of latex will take a very long time to dry. Latex has poor memory, so if you stretch it, it will not completely return to its original shape. Latex tears easily and does not flex as well as silicone, foam latex, or gelatin. Liquid latex contains a lot of ammonia, and it can be pretty harsh to your throat and lungs.

Foam latex

Foam latex is also relatively inexpensive, but it is a nightmare to work with. You need several pieces of equipment such as kitchen mixers and ovens that you can never use for food again. It is very difficult to mix, and it is sensitive to several environmental factors, including ambient temperature and humidity. Foam latex also gives off toxic fumes as it cures. Foam latex does move and flex very well, and can be colored with just about anything, but I would opt for silicone over foam latex in every instance if possible.

■ Gelatin

Gelatin has been used for a long time in the industry. It is more expensive than latex, but less expensive than silicone.

Pros Gelatin allergies are nearly as rare as silicone allergies. If used carefully by an experienced makeup artist, gelatin can be applied directly to the skin and sculpted into realistic wounds. It can be poured into molds and is ready to be pulled as soon as it is cool. It can be intrinsically colored; it is also easy to extrinsically color. Blending edges can be melted away with witch hazel to seamlessly blend them into the skin. Gelatin will become softer as it warms to the actor's body temperature and better displays the properties of flesh. Finally, gelatin can be remelted if a casting comes out poorly.

Cons Gelatin is very hot while still in its liquid form, so care must be taken when applying it to the skin. Gelatin will melt under hot light or in the summer sun and heat.

■ Dermawax

Dermawax is also known as morticians' wax. It is a material that can be easily shaped and blended into the skin. It is not a permanent material by any stretch of the imagination, because it does not dry and stays permanently flexible. It can easily be colored if sealed with a flexible plastic sealer or latex. Dermawax is an excellent choice if an actor needs some type of basic injury and there is no time to sculpt or cast a wound.

■ Alcohol-Activated Makeup

Alcohol-activated (AA) makeup is an excellent material. It is a dry cake that activates with ninety-nine percent isopropyl alcohol. Ninety-one percent or ninety-three percent isopropyl will work, but not as well—the concentration of isopropyl is not high enough to completely dissolve the material.

The best part about AA makeup is that with each spray of alcohol, you are sterilizing the palette, but keep a cup of alcohol on hand to clean and sterilize the brushes between each use.

To remove AA makeup, you can use more alcohol, most commercial makeup removers, soap and water (plus a lot of scrubbing), or even shaving cream. (I was skeptical about this until I tried it on myself, and it really works.)

01 / Alcohol-activated makeup will not run and smear from sweat like greasepaints will. This was a ninety-degree day and he looked just as good—or bad—by the end of the filming day.

Pros AA makeup is waterproof, and it will stay on until you take it off or it wears off the skin. AA makeup won't smudge and can be applied translucent or opaque, typically with a brush, because sponges tend to absorb a lot of material and can be wasteful. AA makeup can be easily blended. It is expensive, but it will last a long time. Liquid colors can be purchased to replace the dry cake when a color is empty.

Cons The fumes from ninety-nine percent isopropyl can be very harsh, and AA makeup can be uncomfortable if applied near the eyes. Sometimes the alcohol can burn or irritate the skin. Telesis makes a gelled alcohol that greatly cuts down on the alcohol smell and burning sensations.

■ Greasepaint

Greasepaint is an oil-based makeup. It can be applied with a sponge, brush, your fingers, or any applicator you happen to have on hand. Greasepaint blends very well and can be applied as opaque as you need it, though it tends to crack or look artificial if applied too thickly.

Greasepaint needs to be set with a translucent powder. If you don't set the makeup, you run the risk of it melting under hot lights, running from perspiration, or smudging. However, greasepaint will still smudge relatively easily, even if you do set it. The flip side is that it also washes off easily with soap and water.

Greasepaint is an excellent option for application near the eyes and is my first choice for drawing on veins.

Equipment

There are several types of tools, equipment, and basic applicators that you should have on hand when getting ready to apply makeup and prosthetic appliances. The most important are brushes, sponges, craft sticks, and cotton-tipped applicators, although there are many other pieces of equipment that you may find useful.

■ Brushes

First and foremost, you need brushes. Makeup and artist brushes can be ridiculously expensive, particularly when you consider that it's likely they'll be ruined by the end of the filming day. However, you can buy an economy pack containing twenty-five assorted brushes, including a couple of chip brushes and sponge brushes, for around five dollars at local craft stores. You may also get lucky and find cheap makeup kits at the dollar store. These kits usually have a powder brush and a few assorted makeup applicators. You'll need to clean and sterilize your brushes each time you use them.

01 / No matter how hard you try to clean your brushes, a lot of the materials effects artists use will never come out of them. Cheap art brushes are the way to go.

■ Sponges

You will need plenty of sponges and makeup wedges. All of the following sponges can be ripped, shredded, or cut to achieve a myriad of different textures and effects.

The downside of using sponges is that they tend to soak up a lot of liquid makeup and can potentially be wasteful.

Wedge sponges are great for general use. Make sure you get the nonlatex variety. Latex-free is always a good choice, because many people have a latex allergy. You can pick them up at pharmacies and beauty supply stores, but I always go back to the dollar store first.

Red-rubber sponges are great for texture and the application of makeup to large areas of the body. They are a bit more expensive than wedges but last considerably longer and can be cleaned and reused. These sponges are not as common as the nonlatex wedges, but you can still find them at most pharmacies.

Stipple sponges are the most important sponges in your kit. There is no better sponge for texturing and blending colors. Stipple sponges are great for creating stubble or rashes and abrasions. They are available

with different pore sizes and in different densities. You can find them at most costume shops and some beauty supply stores.

Natural sea sponges are another excellent tool. They can give an organic texture to your makeup application that you would never be able to achieve otherwise.

Everyday **household sponges** can also come in handy. They come in a multitude of textures and densities and are always inexpensive.

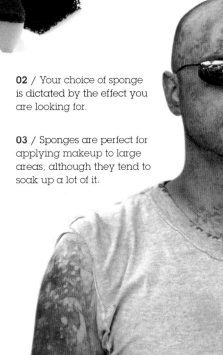

02 / Your choice of sponge is dictated by the effect you are looking for.

03 / Sponges are perfect for applying makeup to large areas, although they tend to soak up a lot of it.

01 / This is before we started filming for the day, so it is as organized as an on-set makeup table will ever be. Notice the red rubber sponge, household sponges, and container full of brushes, craft sticks, and swabs.

■ Craft Sticks and Cotton-Tipped Applicators

You will need some Popsicle sticks (craft sticks) or tongue depressors for a variety of purposes, including using them as palette knives, mixing silicone, sculpting waxes and clays, and even to apply globs of scab blood to an actor. You can get craft sticks or tongue depressors from most craft stores or surgical supply stores.

Cotton-tipped applicators come in handy. They are like cotton swabs, only longer, not as

02 / Cotton-tipped applicators are one of the most useful, yet least expensive, tools in your kit.

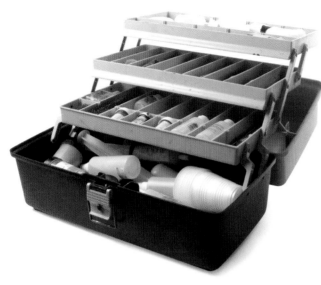

03 / Tackle boxes make excellent makeup cases. They are usually cheaper than dedicated makeup cases, but they are also normally bigger and have just as many divided spaces for your supplies.

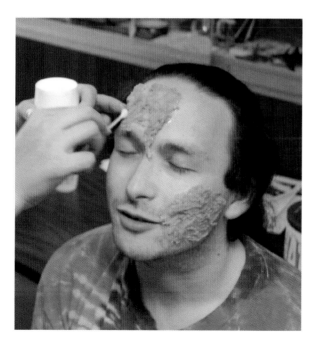

04 / The cotton swab is great for getting adhesive beneath the edges of an appliance.

soft, and only have the cotton at one end. You can get them at many hobby or craft stores, or buy them in bulk from the surgical supply stores. They are excellent for applying adhesive beneath the delicate edge of a prosthetic appliance.

■ Other Equipment

You will need a bag or a case to keep all of your brushes, sponges, and applicators clean. Many people like to use a cheap toolbox or fishing-tackle box. Tackle boxes have all of the dividers to keep your applicators organized and clean. You can invest in a brush roll case, or simply leave the brushes in the plastic packaging they come in until you need one.

A plastic folding table can also be useful, because the makeup crew always seems to need more workspace, no matter how much space they already have. It is a good idea to bring a few folding chairs with you to the set. You want to keep the actors comfortable, and they usually prefer sitting instead of standing when complicated makeup is being applied.

Have a hair dryer, hand mirror, paper towels, facial tissues, tweezers, cuticle scissors (the only scissors I have found that will cut the thin edges of a silicone appliance), paper cups, foam plates, cotton balls, talc, chip brushes, and nitrile gloves on hand. Nitrile gloves are generally more resistant to chemical solvents and punctures than latex or vinyl gloves, will not irritate latex allergies, and are far easier to put on than latex gloves, especially for people like me that have very large hands.

choosing a Look For your zombies

Before you start making up your undead horde, you should take time to think about how they will look. Anyone can come up with a generic zombie, but coming up with a look that reflects the cause of the zombie outbreak and undertaking a bit of research into realism will both focus your makeup and effects designs and add to the quality and individuality of your movie.

■ Origins of Species

You may decide that zombies caused by a radiological event may look different from corpses reanimated by the forces of darkness. Or a biological event such as a virus or some kind of disease may result in a completely different zombie than one who was raised by voodoo. Of course, this is all completely open to individual interpretation—over the following pages you'll discover just a few of the possible approaches.

Before jumping in feet first, the production team and the makeup and effects artists should sit down together to figure out exactly where your zombies are coming from. Are they going to be runny and oozing, are they going to be desiccated, mummified beasts, or are they going to be mutated things that barely look human? Then you need to figure out what their wardrobe is going to be like. Are the zombie's clothes going to be tattered funeral vestments, covered in the dirt of the graves from which they crawled, or blood-spattered clothes that the shambling corpses were wearing at the moment of death?

Once you have answered these questions, you can start covering your actors in all kinds of slime and other nastiness.

01 / Once you've gained experience, liquid makeup and greasepaint alone can produce a convincing zombie without the need for creating prosthetic appliances.

CASE STUDY ONE: **VIRUSES AND BACTERIAL INFECTIONS**

Viruses and bacterial infections can cause any number of horrible things to befall the human body. It has been said that "The single greatest threat to man's continued existence on earth is the virus." The man who said this was a Nobel Prize-winning biologist, so I think I'd trust his judgment. Hemorrhagic fevers such as those caused by the Ebola virus can be up to ninety percent fatal. Ebola can make it look like a patient's internal organs were taken out, run through a blender, and then poured back in through his or her bodily orifices. Necrotizing fasciitis (NF) is caused by relatively common microscopic bacteria that surrounds us every day. You can see the effects of the bacteria eating the living tissue of an infected person. If NF does not outright kill a person, there will be massive tissue damage and probable amputation of infected limbs.

Zombies caused by bacterial or viral infection might be very "juicy." The colors typical of infection can run the gamut, but we will typically use greens, browns, and other earth tones and then build the redness and inflammation on top of that. Pustules, blisters, and running sores are the way to go—you can never have too much puss. There may be a lot of redness and swelling around the mucous membranes. NF can cause deep black fissures where living flesh used to be.

02 / Germs are nasty. That will teach him to shave his back with a razor he found in a gas station bathroom.

CASE STUDY TWO: **RADIATION**

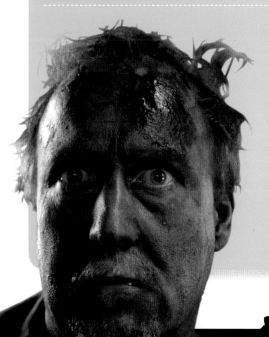

Radiation causes all kinds of unpleasant things to happen to a body. Radiation burns can cause redness, swelling, and blistering. Irradiated skin can slip or flake off the body. Severe cancers and growths can develop in a very short time after exposure. Mutations run rampant in the offspring of those exposed to dangerously high levels.

Radioactive zombies might have a lot of pink and red inflammation, peeling skin, yellow blisters, and blackened burns. There may be extensive loss of hair. There might be large tumors or severe keloidal scarring.

03 / He blames the radiation every day for the hair loss.

CASE STUDY THREE: **REANIMATED**

My favorite zombies are those that have been reanimated, perhaps by a scientist or by the bite of another zombie. If you're going for the latter, you have the added fun of an almost infinite number of gruesome injuries, bites, and scratches to choose from. A deep zombie bite might have rough jagged edges and torn skin sticking out. I like to make the zombie wounds ooze with a blackish red ichor. Sometimes I'll even rig it up so a chunk of meat will fall out of the wound. In some movies, the zombies aren't reanimated by another zombie, but instead by science.

Go crazy with this kind of undead. Maybe a zombie tore the villager's arm off and drooled all over the stump. If you think you can make the stump convincing, then give it a try.

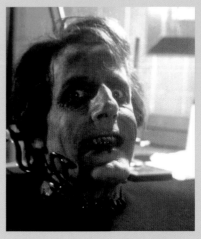

01 / In *Reanimator* (1985), Herbert West was responsible for bringing his share of zombies back to "life."

■ Realism

Once you've chosen the origins of your zombie outbreak, it's worth doing some research to make your makeup and effects realistic for your audience. Realism is important. I have a collection of medical reference works and similar books, and all kinds of anatomical charts and references, which I use for guidance when deciding if a gag will look real. (I have to warn people about those books before they browse through my book collection.)

Your zombies are still the people or animals that they were before becoming reanimated corpses, and knowing how everything works

"under the hood" will help you create some disturbing makeup illusions that are convincing to the audience. Whether you are creating a zombie or some other monster, basic anatomical principles still apply. If your hideous fiend walks, it will need some kind of bone and muscle support system. If it has hands and fingers, there needs to be some kind of connective tissue that will allow the monster to grab its victim.

Your story might call for a zombie to have died and become reanimated in a desert, the frozen arctic, or in a muddy swamp. Having an idea of what all of these environments will do to a corpse should help to point you in the right

direction when designing the makeup effect. The desert zombie will most likely be a lot less juicy than the zombie that just crawled out of the swamp.

The last zombie movie I worked on required blisters and sores of all kinds. I did an Internet search on pustules and found more images than I really ever wanted to see. However, as a result, my prosthetic pustules looked like the real thing.

There are some basic things that happen to all animals after they die: blood stops pumping; the immune system stops fighting all of the bad bacteria in the body; and bloating occurs. I think it is a good idea to know what all of this does to a body and how it looks. Knowing what livor mortis is and how it would look if your zombie died while lying on a storm drain can only add to the quality of your makeup.

02 / Accessories can make the zombie. Bloody wardrobe, a knife sticking out of the back or even a DVD embedded in the skull are all nice finishing touches.

Blood gags and bullet wounds

Blood gags (special effects) and bullet hits are an important part of most zombie movies. When the sheriff gets his jugular torn out, blood really should spray. This is where the compressors, garden sprayers, syringes, and all kinds of pumps come in. I have even seen guys using water pistols and squirt guns.

01 / The tube coming out of the prosthetic is attached to a syringe full of blood.

> ## Blood Gel
>
> *Blood gel is one of the best tools you'll have in your makeup kit. It is a very thick, sticky, almost sculptable blood-color material. A dark line of greasepaint under a streak of blood gel will, fairly convincingly, create the illusion of a deep cut. Use whatever you have on hand to apply the gel—the end of a brush would work, but I use tongue depressors or Popsicle sticks.*

■ Oozing and Spraying Blood

To create this type of blood gag, you'll need a length of oxygen tubing or aquarium tubing—the diameter of the tubing depends on the gag itself and the amount of goo you want to ooze—fake blood, and a device to pump blood out of the tube.

Garden sprayers are a good choice for arterial spray or when you need high volume of goo.

Inexpensive garden sprayers have hand pumps on them and can be pressurized to a fairly high PSI. They come with squeeze triggers and all kinds of modular parts that make it easy to control the amount and duration of liquid pumped during a blood gag. However, you'll have to play around with the viscosity of the blood. Too thick and it will ooze instead

of spray; too thin and it will lack opacity and look like pink water on whatever it splatters against.

Big syringes are good for a more controlled oozing. I get boxes of 60cc syringes from the surgical supply store; I bought a big eight-ounce surgical steel syringe on eBay; and I even found a giant "syringe" at a discount hardware chain that holds a full quart of whatever nasty slime I decide to fill it with.

Once you've chosen your pump and got your fake blood and tubing, you'll need to work out how to get the blood to spray out of the wound. This can be a tricky task—while running a piece under the actor's wardrobe to the injury site is easy, camouflaging the tubing so the camera can't see it is another matter altogether.

The easiest way to do it is to cheat the angle by keeping the obvious tube on the opposite side of the actor from the camera. Actually, you can get away with a lot of gags this way, but sometimes you just need to see gore spraying directly out of the wound. One way to do it is to build the blood tubing directly into the prosthetic appliance, as shown in the diagram below.

Making a Blood Gag

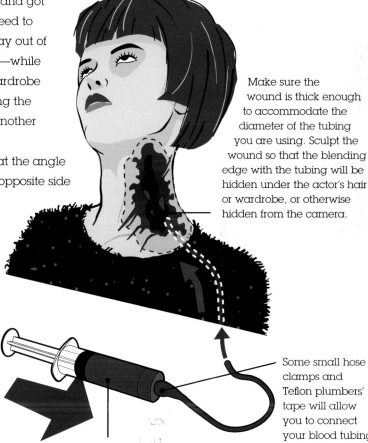

Make sure the wound is thick enough to accommodate the diameter of the tubing you are using. Sculpt the wound so that the blending edge with the tubing will be hidden under the actor's hair or wardrobe, or otherwise hidden from the camera.

Some small hose clamps and Teflon plumbers' tape will allow you to connect your blood tubing to just about any kind of pump.

With the appliance in place, rig up a pump or syringe to fill the line with blood or goo and make it ooze.

Connectors

You can "step up" the size of your tubing to fit over whatever nozzle your pump has. You will find a variety of tubing at the hardware store, and it will typically come in standard sizes. The outside diameter of one tube will match the inside diameter of another. Using a few clamps, you can match up just about any nozzle to almost any blood tube you will ever need.

■ Bullet Hits

Garden sprayers are not only good for creating arterial sprays, they're also a great choice for bullet hits. It is comparatively simple to make a gag with one (see right). You'll need a hose with a larger diameter capable of handling a higher PSI. For a bullet hit, you want all of the blood to burst out at once, rather than ooze.

01 / Forty to fifty PSI of pneumatic pressure can send a blast of goo up to twenty yards. Go ahead, try for distance!

You can also use an air compressor with an attached air storage tank. It works basically the same way as the empty garden sprayer, but you have better control over the pressure and it will be easier to repeat the gag with nearly identical results if the director wants another take, or you can adjust the pressure if the first take was not quite right.

Making a Bullet Hit

Step 1: Take a length of plastic tubing, plug up one end, and bore a hole into one side on the same end that is plugged. That hole is where the blood will come out to simulate the bullet hit. Cover the hole with plastic wrap, or plug it with a bit of sponge.

Step 2: Fill the tube with goo and tape it to the actor beneath his wardrobe. Connect the filled tube to an empty garden sprayer that you have pumped to the point that the seals are getting ready to burst.

Step 3: On action, squeeze the trigger. All of the potential energy stored in the sprayer will force the blood out of the tube in a pretty impressive simulation of a bullet impact.

■ Meat and Gore

Chances are that you'll want some body parts, severed limbs, and gnawed-upon corpses to litter the scene. Besides the makeup, blood gags, and bullet hits, meaty people chunks will go a long way in selling the illusion that the undead are walking around and eating people.

Body parts and random chunks of meat are pretty easy to make. Liquid latex is cheap and will be the primary ingredient in just about any body part you'll need to create. Spray insulation foam in a can is invaluable. Basically, anything around the house that you can make look gross and chewy is something you can use. I've purchased resin replicas of human bones on eBay. With a bit of latex and some paint, they can be made to look pretty disgusting. I also make it a point to browse the costume shops the day after Halloween, when most of their stock is on sale. I can get all kinds of severed limbs, heads, and bags of bones that can be made to look realistic with a little bit of work and a splash of fake blood.

02 / Latex meat is easy to make, looks good on camera, and holds onto whatever goop you cover it with.

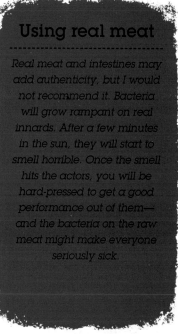

Using real meat

Real meat and intestines may add authenticity, but I would not recommend it. Bacteria will grow rampant on real innards. After a few minutes in the sun, they will start to smell horrible. Once the smell hits the actors, you will be hard-pressed to get a good performance out of them— and the bacteria on the raw meat might make everyone seriously sick.

03 / You don't have to use real blood and bones. Resin bones are quite expensive, but you can't beat the results once you've added some nastiness over them.

makeup and prosthetics

Now it really is time for the fun part—making up your cast. Over the next few pages, I'll take you through various zombie makeups that my colleagues and I have created for our movies. I'll talk about possible color themes and cover some basic prosthetic appliances. I'll even show you a step-by-step construction of a full facial prosthetic appliance.

■ Zombies with No Prosthetics

If your budget is small and time is short, it is possible to create a convincing zombie using absolutely no prosthetic wounds or appliances.

Materials List
- Cream or crème makeup wheels—we use Ben Nye or Kryolan.
- Liquid makeup—we use Mehron.
- Alcohol-activated makeup—we use W. M. Creations or Premier Products.
- Blood gel.
- Sponges and brushes.

If the look you are striving for requires it, apply a cream or liquid makeup base color to the entire facial area using a sponge.

Using a brush, darken the sunken areas of the face—the corners of the eyes, the nasal-labial fold, the temples, and beneath the jawline—with a darker color.

Accent the natural folds and wrinkles in the skin using an even darker shade and a smaller

01 / Liquid makeup and greasepaints work well when used together. Add a little dab of blood gel and you have yourself a zombie.

brush. Highlight the raised areas of the face such as the brow and cheekbones using a lighter color than the foundation tone.

Create the illusion of injury and trauma with more makeup and blood gels.

Draw in some of the details such as veins and blisters with a brush or corner of a sponge. This will tie the whole look together.

■ Zombies with Prosthetic Wounds

I like to make my own zombie prosthetics out of silicone. To create your prosthetic appliances, you'll need to sculpt all of the wounds and gruesome injuries that you want to apply to your actors. You'll then need to create a mold of those sculpts, and you use this mold to create the appliances themselves.

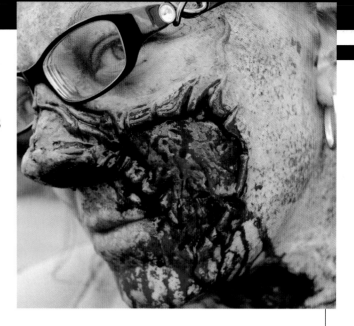

02 / *We couldn't really rip out a piece of the actor's cheek, so I thought the prosthetic would be the next best thing.*

Preparing Silicone for Prosthetic Appliances

There are several methods and materials to get a good prosthetic appliance, including gel-filled appliances, gelatin, and latex. I'll tell you one way to go about it, which is the way I do it. You can research other ways to accomplish the gag and determine what your own preference is.

For making facial prosthetics, I tend to use Polytek's Platsil Gel-10, with prosthetic deadener added. Prosthetic deadener softens silicone to make it better simulate the movement of real flesh. The more deadener you add, the softer the silicone will get. Alternatives you could try include Platsil Gel-00, which is a newer product that exhibits the same properties as deadened Gel-10 in a straight one-to-one ratio, or Smooth-On's products such as Dragon Skin FX-Pro.

First, measure out into separate containers one part A, one part B, and about one-and-a-half parts deadener. Knowing exactly how much to add takes practice—use too much deadener and the silicone will become very soft and tacky. Add a very small amount of the

flesh pigment to part B and mix it thoroughly. A little will go a long way.

Add the flocking to the other component. Flocking is a small, thread-like material that will not dissolve but remains suspended in the silicone. It'll look like blood vessels and mottling under the skin in the finished appliance. Again, knowing exactly how much you need to use will come with practice. One of the greatest assets of silicone is its translucence. You don't want to overpigment it. Too much color and you run the risk of the silicone looking like a slice of deli ham.

When you're ready to make your appliance, mix part B and the deadener completely, until there is a uniform color to the material. Avoid "whipping"—you don't want to trap any air bubble in the silicone. Next, mix in part A, using the same care to avoid air bubbles.

At this point, you'll have about three to eight minutes to get the silicone into whatever mold you are using. The exact time depends on the silicone you use and the temperature—silicone will cure faster the warmer it is.

Materials List

- Nonsulfur Polymer (NSP) clay
—I use Chavant and Van Aken.
- Mold material—I use
Ultracal-30 (UC-30) gypsum
cement.
- A nonporous, relatively
smooth surface on which
to sculpt.
- Something to make "mold
walls"—Lego and Megablocks
are awesome for this. I have
also used foam board (the
insulation kind), cut to the size
I needed and taped or hot
glued together.
- Release agent to make it
easier to get the clay out of the
mold later—petroleum jelly
works fine, but there are also
dedicated products such as
Epoxy Parfilm.

Step 1: First, you'll need to sculpt your appliances. Sulfur-free oil-based clay or NSP are ideal materials for creating your appliances. Avoid sulfur clays because, by doing so, you won't have to worry about inhibition if you use silicone in the mold. Sculpting is an art that takes years of practice, and teaching how to sculpt is beyond the scope of this book, but the more you sculpt, the easier it will become. Sculpt all of your wounds on some type of nonporous tray. In this example, I am sculpting on a piece of tempered glass from an old coffee table.

Step 2: Once you've sculpted some wounds, it is time to prepare them to make the negative mold. There are many ways to make the negative mold; the following method for making UC-30 "box" molds is one of the simplest. Make a mold wall around the sculpts on the nonporous tray using the Legos or foam board. When constructing the box, leave a bit of space between the wall and the sculpts. Make the wall at least an inch or so higher than the height of the tallest sculpt.

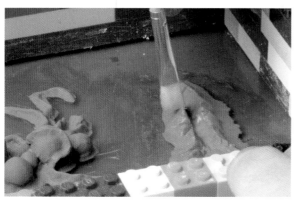

Step 3: Next, apply a release to the surfaces of the sculpts and the tray by brushing a very thin layer of petroleum jelly over them, being careful not to apply it too thick and obscuring some of the details or too rough and damaging any of the details. You can then spray them with a release such as Epoxy Parfilm. This will make it easier to get all of the clay out of the mold later

Step 4: Prepare the Ultracal-30 (UC-30). As a general rule, you'll need three times as much gypsum powder as water. Figuring out how much Ultracal and water you will need is a skill that comes with practice. Your best bet is to eye how much water you think will fill the mold walls, and use just a bit less. Using a flour sifter, slowly sift the gypsum powder into the water (don't pour the water into the cement) until the container that the water is in looks like a dry lake bed. Once it reaches this state, use a tongue depressor or a plastic spoon to mix the cement and water—the consistency should be somewhere between whole milk and heavy cream.

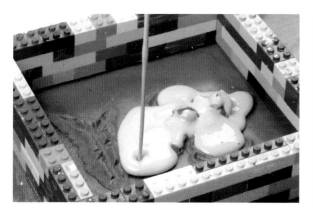

Step 5: Next, pour the mixed cement into your mold wall. Usually, I'll pour a little bit in and use a disposable "acid brush" to paint the cement into the deepest detail areas. Then I'll slowly pour UC-30 into the mold, making sure the cement is at least ⅜ to ½ inch (0.75 to 1.25 cm) above the highest point of the sculpt. The cement will start to get very hot; wait until the stone is almost back to room temperature before you continue.

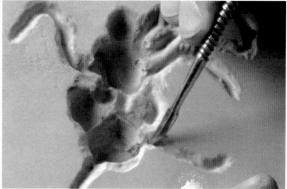

Step 6: Once the mold has cooled, pull the mold walls away and separate the hardened block from the tray of sculpts. Remove all of the remaining clay from the negative mold and the tray. Use sculpting tools, small flat-head screwdrivers, or whatever you have on hand that won't damage the stone. You can use naphtha and an acid brush.

Step 7: Next, make a blank using the same mold walls that you used to make the negative mold. Mix up some more Ultracal-30, then pour it into the mold walls on the clean tray. This will give you a smooth stone blank. When it comes time to make the prosthetic piece, I'll put the casting material in to the negative mold and then clamp the "blank" to it. This ensures that the edges of the piece are onion-skin thin. Of course, I do not make the blank for every mold.

Step 8: Apply a release to the negative (see step 3) and, if using them, the blank halves of the mold. Use very thin coats of the same combination of petroleum jelly and a spray release that you used in step 3. I tend to over-release the negative and under-release the blank. Mix up a batch of silicone (see page 71). Slowly pour the silicone into the negative half of the mold at its lowest point. Using a brush or tongue depressor, make sure that the silicone has filled in all of the detail and has not trapped any air bubbles. Fill the mold so that the silicone completely fills all of the negative space.

Step 9: Strap or clamp the blank half of the mold to the negative. Any excess material will be forced out the sides of the mold. Consult the data sheet or instructions that came with the silicone (or whatever casting material you chose). The data sheet will tell you how long you need to wait for the material to cure. For silicone, I will wait for at least thirty to forty minutes—longer if it is colder, less if it is warm. Sometimes, I'll set the mold under a lamp to gradually heat the stone. It helps the silicone cure faster and softens the release to make pulling the piece easier.

Step 10: You have now waited long enough—you can pull the appliance. It should come out easily if you released the mold well enough. Work slowly. There will be a vacuum holding the whole thing together, and it might be frustrating if the mold does not immediately come apart. You'll hear the silicone separating from the stone and a sucking sound as air rushes into the deep recesses of the sculpts. You now will get your first look at your set of appliances.

■ Full Facial Prosthetics

The most expensive and time-consuming of the makeup applications you can do involves full facial prosthetics. A lot of time and effort is involved, and you will need to decide on the look, create the sculpt, and make sure the production team is aware of the time it will take to accomplish the gag. Make sure you carefully read all of the instructions and safety warnings for the materials you are about to use. There are also a lot of tutorials online—watch a few of them to make sure you understand the materials you'll be using.

Making a full facial prosthetic involves several major stages: taking a life cast of the actor's face; using that cast to make a stone copy; sculpting your horrifying creation on the stone copy; making a mold of the sculpt; and, finally, using that mold to cast the final prosthetic. It's a lot of work, so take your time to get it right.

01 / A prosthetic appliance made from a life cast will fit the actor's face perfectly and will move seamlessly with every expression he or she makes.

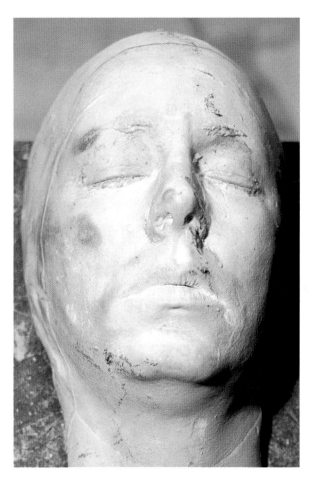

Materials List

- ½ to 1 lb (225 to 450 g) alginate (some heads are bigger than others).
- Two or three rolls of 6-inch (15-cm) quick-set plaster bandages, and one roll of 3-inch (7.5-cm) bandages.
- Adhesive-backed weather stripping to create a clear, sharp line to know where your life cast should stop.
- Bald cap to keep alginate out of the hair.
- Ultracal-30 and sulfur-free oil-based clay or NSP—the amount of each depends on the prosthetic you are making.
- Petroleum jelly.
- Epoxy Parfilm.
- Old clothes.
- Drop cloths and plastic sheeting.

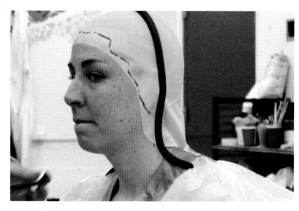

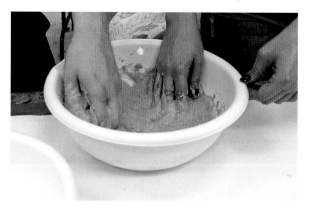

Step 1: Making a life cast can be a little messy, so make sure your model is wearing old clothes and sitting comfortably. You can cover the actor's body with plastic sheeting to protect his or her clothing. You might also want to cover the floor just in case. Apply a bald cap to the actor. A bald cap will serve to make the life cast neater and will keep the alginate out of the actor's hair. In this example, the artists at AnomalyFX used lengths of adhesive weather stripping to define exactly where they wanted the edge of the life cast to be.

Step 2: Once the actor is completely prepped, mix the alginate. The Dick Smith recipe is one 7-ounce (210-ml) cup of alginate (sifted, not packed) to one 7-ounce (210-ml) cup of water. You can double, triple, quadruple this recipe ... but use the 7-ounce (210-ml) cups. Dick Smith is the master, so I trust his recipe. The colder the water used, the longer the working time will be. Once thoroughly mixed, the alginate will have about the viscosity of peanut butter.

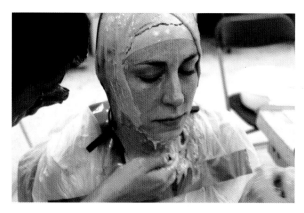

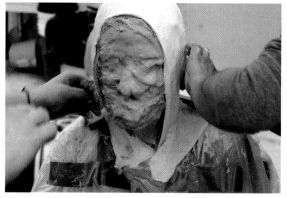

Step 3: Apply the alginate all over the area within the weather stripping. Have the model close her eyes and cover her entire face, leaving the nose area until last. Use care around the nose because you don't want to cut off the actor's air supply. You can place a drinking straw in each nostril if you or the actor is worried. You have to work fast, however, because alginate will set in around five to ten minutes.

Step 4: Cured alginate is "floppy." You need to encase it in a rigid shell. This is where you apply the plaster bandages. Take your rolls of plaster bandage and cut them into strips. I typically use strips about 3 feet (1 m) long then folded in half, giving me a double layer about 1½ feet (50 cm) long. Dip the bandage in warm water and use your fingers to spread the plaster throughout the whole bandage, at the same time squeezing the excess water out. Cover the entire surface of the alginate, making sure you overlap and provide extra support to the nose area. The bandages will set in about five to ten minutes.

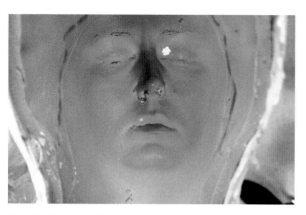

Step 5: After the plaster bandage has hardened, you can remove the entire mold from the model. You now have an exact replica of the model's face, only in negative relief.

Step 6: The next stage is to make the positive half of the mold, the copy of the actor's face, using Ultracal-30. Before mixing the stone, plug up the nostrils on the mold with a piece of clay so that the cement does not simply pour out of the nostril holes. Mix the UC-30 (see page 73, step 4), and slowly pour it into the alginate. Use an acid brush to make sure that cement gets in to all of the detail areas, and tap the mold a few times to try to release any trapped air bubbles.

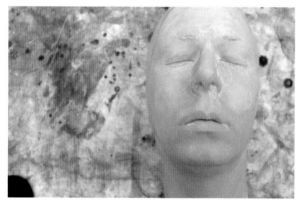

Step 7: The stone copy of the model's face is ready to be pulled from the alginate mold once the cement starts to cool. The stone will not be completely hardened until it has totally cooled, and it may still feel almost damp for a few days. Once the stone copy is pulled, you can use sculpting tools, files, or sanding blocks to remove any imperfections. Imperfections and bubbles are common around the nose, mouth, and corners of the eyes, and any area of the cast that had hair or stubble. You should now have an exact stone replica of your model, which will be the base on which you sculpt the appliance.

Step 8: Before you start, drill a couple of registration keys in an area of the face that will not affect the sculpt. Registration keys ensure the mold halves will line up perfectly. Now just start adding the clay. The only rules you need to follow are to make sure the edges blend in smoothly to the face and to avoid undercuts. Undercuts are caused by protruding areas of the sculpt that will lead to recesses forming in the negative mold. The undercuts will cause the mold to lock together as if it was a jigsaw puzzle.

Step 9: After your sculpt is complete and you have eliminated all of the undercuts, you will need to make the negative mold out of UC-30. For simplicity's sake, we'll make another UC-30 "box" mold. Start by making a mold wall around the sculpture. Use foam board for this one, because you would need a lot of Legos for a wall this big. When constructing the box, leave about 2 inches (5 cm) on all sides of the face or sculpt.

Step 10: Next, apply a release to the sculpt in the same way you did before (see page 76, step 3), only make sure that you have covered every single inch of exposed stone. If you don't release the stone absolutely completely, the new cement you pour when you make the negative will bond to it and lock the mold. Once the mold wall is built and you have applied the release agent, all you need to do is to cover the entire thing in UC-30 in the same way we covered the generic wound sculpts. Pour slowly and make sure you don't trap any air bubbles in the detailed areas. Now just let it cool so that it's almost back to room temperature.

Step 11: Now is the moment of truth. It is time to pull the mold halves apart. Pull the mold walls away, and carefully tip the mold on its side. You may need to use a screwdriver or other utensil to pry the halves apart. Just take it easy and go slowly. You have to remove all of the clay that you added to the face and clean the clay from the negative mold. Clean the mold using sculpting tools, small flat-head screwdrivers, or a similar object, taking care not to damage the stone. Alternatively, use naphtha and an acid brush.

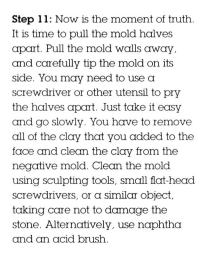

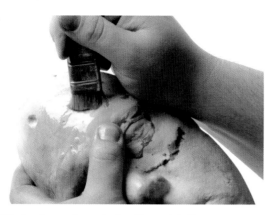

Step 12: Apply a release to the life cast in the same way you did before (see page 73, step 3). Mix up a batch of silicone (see page 71). Slowly pour the silicone into the negative half of the mold at its lowest point. Using a brush or tongue depressor, make sure that the silicone has filled in all of the detail and has not trapped any air bubbles. The silicone will slump to the lowest point in the mold, but that is fine.

Step 13: Insert the positive half of the mold, the face, into the negative half. With big box molds, I will set the whole thing on the floor and stand on it to seat the face securely and squeeze all of the excess silicone into the run-off sections of the mold such as the pry points. Set a heavy weight to hold things in place. Go grab a sandwich—you will have to wait at least 30 to 40 minutes, depending on the silicone you used, the thickness of the mold, and the ambient temperature.

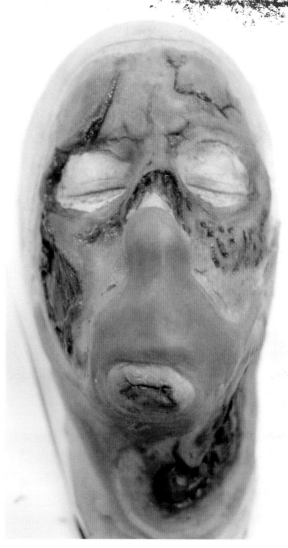

Step 14: You are now ready to separate the mold and pull the appliance. Just as there is with the simple prosthetics mold, there will be a vacuum holding it together, so work slowly and carefully to pull it apart. With the pry points I sculpt into the molds, I have plenty of places to put a screwdriver to get some leverage to pry them apart. You now have a facial prosthetic ready for coloring and applying to your actor.

■ Coloring and Applying Partial and Full-Facial Prosthetics

You did the life cast, you sculpted your zombie, and, with luck, you have a prosthetic pulled from that mold that is ready to be cleaned, painted, and finally applied to the actor.

Materials List

- Ninety-nine percent isopropyl or acetone.
- Small quantity of silicone.
- Alcohol-activated makeup and greasepaint.
- Translucent powder.

Wash the appliance in ninety-nine percent isopropyl or acetone to get all of the release agents off the piece. Removing the release agents will help your color adhere to the piece. Also, there is a possibility that the release agents might irritate your actor's skin.

Color the appliance using a mixture of colorant added to small quantities of parts A and B of your silicone. Thin the mixture with naphtha to a paintable consistency. Apply this in thin, layered washes to achieve a measure of opacity. Color in the details of the piece, making sure that all of the work you did on the sculpt will stand out.

You are now ready to stick the appliance to your actor and blend it in. The main reason for using silicone as a base for the colorant is that nothing sticks to silicone better than more silicone. This is also why I use platinum-based silicones as an adhesive when applying the prosthetics to your actor's skin.

01 / The full-facial appliance glued down with silicone, the edges blended, and a cohesive color applied to the entire facial area along with some fake blood and blood gel.

Smaller prosthetics are easy to apply. Mix together a tiny amount of parts A and B. Work quickly now, because this minute amount of silicone will cure very quickly. Next, work out where you want to place the appliance on the actor, then coat the back of it with a tiny bit of silicone to within about ⅛ to ¼ inch (3 to 6 mm) from the edge. Press the prosthetic in place, making sure not to roll or fold the edges. Take a swab and a pair of tweezers or forceps and carefully glue down the edges. If your edges are thin enough, they will practically disappear. After a few minutes you'll be ready to blend the wound into the surrounding area (see opposite).

Full-facial prosthetics are slightly trickier, and you'll need to apply the silicone in stages. With a swab or similar applicator, apply a thin film of wet silicone to the center of the appliance. Press

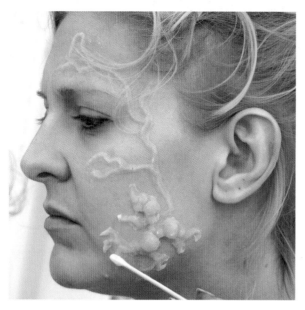

02 / Use the swab to go underneath the edge of the appliance and roll out the edge, away from the center of the piece. This will help the edges lay flat.

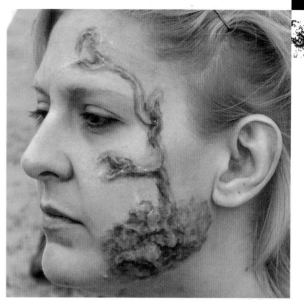

03 / Once your appliance is glued down, you can start coloring and blending. These colors will blend into the skin on the actor's face once the rest of the makeup is applied.

the piece into place on your actor. Continue to spread the silicone on the piece, working from the center outward. The silicone will cure as you work because of the body heat of the actor. For the larger, full-facial prosthetics, you will probably need to mix a few of the tiny batches of parts A and B in order to completely glue down the piece.

Start blending in the edges of your appliance. The better your mold technique, the thinner the edges of the piece will be, which will make blending the edges easier. Again, silicone is translucent, so if you didn't go overboard on the pigment or the flocking, the edges should already be almost invisible. To completely hide the edges, I'll use a sponge or the tip of my finger to lightly stipple silicone around the perimeter of the appliance. Soon, the edge will vanish. You can lightly tint this final stipple coat of silicone to better blend the edges.

Blend in the appliance by using a combination of alcohol-activated makeup, liquid makeup, and greasepaint. Using a stipple sponge or a chip brush, stipple AA makeup on the edges of the appliance and out onto the actor's skin. Ninety-nine percent isopropyl can be pretty harsh, so it shouldn't be used around the actor's eyes and mucous membranes—instead, use greasepaint or liquids.

To tie everything together, use a toothbrush or trimmed chip brush to "flick" AA makeup over the whole appliance, making sure to include the area around it. This will help to further hide any edges and sell the illusion that the carnage on the actor is authentic.

Once everything is glued down, colored, and blended, you should lightly powder the entire application with a translucent powder to take off any shine and set the greasepaint.

production

Production is going to be the most exciting part of the process. You'll actually be shooting your movie. Production is also going to be the time when you are likely to get a few ulcers and a lot of gray hair, and when you will wish you'd spent more time doing preproduction. It will be an enormous learning experience—you will find out pretty quickly what you did right and what you did wrong.

Final Night and Day

Roll	Scene	Take
	Head shot Lil' Brother	3

Principal photography also promises to be the most fun. You'll go on location, you'll get to see your special effects gags go off, and you'll hear your dialogue performed like the actors mean it. It is exhilarating to be on a movie set, no matter what job you are doing. There are not that many people who do what we do, and it is a rush to know that you are now one of the select few who have the courage to make their own movie.

One of the most important things you have to try to do at this stage is stay on schedule. When filming an independent movie, almost everyone is working on the project when they can. Often your cast and crew will need to make special arrangements to be a part of the movie. To be fair to them, you need to do everything in your power to make your movie in the time you told them it would take.

Always remember that things happen, unforeseen events occur, and it will sometimes seem as though the entire world is conspiring against your movie. Just do the best you can with what you have. Always try to keep a positive attitude. You are steering the ship—if it at least looks like you know where you are going, your cast or crew will be confident in your abilities and will do their best to help you make a decent flick!

01 / KNB EFX did an incredible job on the effects for the TV series *The Walking Dead*, which was first aired in 2010. The enormous popularity of the show has helped to keep zombies prominent in popular culture.

02 / The makers of *Zombieland* (2009) had the resources to use guns and exploding head shots for every zombie, but mixing up the carnage makes for a more interesting movie.

preparation

There are some basic things that need to be done before you are ready to film, and some items that you must remember to take with you to the shoot. This isn't quite preproduction; it's more of a survivor's guide to your first day of principal photography. Some of it is common sense, while some are things that I have run into and have become common sense through experience.

01 / Camera—check. Monitor—check. Stands and tripod—check. Coffee—check. Ok, now you have everything you need for the day and you are ready to start shooting.

Obviously, you will need to remember the camera, tripod, lights, and assorted stands. Make sure you charge up your camera battery the night before you are going to film.

Before leaving for the set, you need to take a quick inventory and pack a "bag of tricks," also known as essential items for yourself and the crew—some of these things you will need, some your DP will need, and some of this stuff everyone else on the set will wind up asking for.

Gaffer's tape This is basically a fancy name for duct tape that doesn't leave a residue. You never know what can happen when you're on set. You may need to tape some cardboard over a window to get the lighting right, or the leg of your tripod may need a quick repair. Even if you just have to tape some cables down to the ground for safety and to keep the PAs from tripping on them and potentially knocking over the camera, gaffer's tape is a necessity.

Clothespins Always pack some spring-loaded clothespins. If you need to attach a colored gel to a light, hold an errant microphone cable out of the way, or even just mark a page of the script, they will come in handy.

Cords and adapters Bring plenty of extension cords, surge protectors, and adapters to plug your grounded cords into nongrounded outlets. You are going to use a lot of power when filming, and you can never be sure if you will have an outlet or two close at hand. An

Checklist

- Gaffer's tape
- Clothespins
- Extension cords, surge protectors, and adapters
- Camera charger and an extra battery (or two)
- Extra storage media for digital files
- Shooting pages of script and notes
- Aspirin, antacids, and sunscreen
- Towels and spare clothes

02 / You'll find gaffer's tape and clothespins are indispensable on set.

01 / Sometimes you know there will be plenty of power. Sometimes you plug in one more light and everything goes black. If you can, plug things in to multiple outlets. If possible, plug things in to separate circuits.

assortment of extension cords and a few multi-outlet surge protectors will let you bring power to where you need it. Sometimes you may find that the location at which you are filming has very old wiring or was just never updated with grounded outlets. The adapters that allow you to plug in to a nongrounded outlet will only cost you about a dollar or two each, but they will save you all kinds of headaches knowing you can plug in wherever you need. Make sure you bring a few extension cords, and always unroll or unravel them before plugging things in.

Batteries and charger Make sure you bring your camera charger and an extra battery if you have one. If you remembered to bring the charger and

Note

On one of my first movies, I let the director use my 100-foot (30-m) reeled extension cord. He plugged 2,500 watts worth of halogen lights, a monitor, and two camera chargers into the surge protector at the end of the cord. The surge protector kept tripping, and he just kept resetting it. He neglected to unroll the cord and it melted all the way through. He ruined my cord, and the short threw the breaker at the house where we were filming.

The moral of the story is, don't allow easily preventable mistakes to disrupt your shoot.

extension cords, you can just shoot while plugged in to AC power or always have a spare battery on the charger. You do not want to be in the middle of an excellent take when your camera runs out of juice.

Storage media Always have extra storage media on hand. If you keep extra DV tapes, SDHC cards, P2 cards, or whatever you're using on hand, you can just switch out the media and keep filming when your "tape" gets full. Swapping out the media is much faster than having to stop production to dump your footage to a computer before you can begin filming again. If your camera records to an internal hard disk drive, you will need to schedule time to dump the footage to free up space. This can coincide with a break for cast and crew. You just need to make sure you back up everything you have dumped after the filming day is done.

Script and shot list Make sure you bring the pages of the script that you plan to shoot and any notes regarding those scenes. Create a shot list

the night before and bring that too. A shot list is a list of the shots you want to get that day, with a brief description of framing and camera angles.

Painkillers Bring some aspirin, because you are likely to get a headache from everyone screaming at you that they don't know what to do. And bring some antacid tablets, because you might get indigestion from inhaling your lunch instead of taking your time to eat.

Towels and spare clothes Taking a cue from Douglas Adams, a towel is a necessity. You can cover with it if cold, dry off with it if wet, kneel on it to get the perfect shot, and use it to clean off blood. And bring a change of clothes and a spare pair of shoes. We have filmed in the rain, the DP has fallen into a pond, and the makeup crew always winds up covered in blood. The ride home is much more comfortable in dry clothes.

Hat and sunscreen I have gone home on more than one occasion with a sunburn. I may look silly in the boonie hat, but the protection is worth it.

02 / Getting blood on your clothes is an occupational hazard when making zombie movies, so make sure you bring a towel and a change of clothes.

Lighting

Nothing makes a low-budget movie look more low-budget than bad lighting. Heavy shadows and grainy images may be the key to a noir film, but you are making a zombie movie. What is the point of spending a big portion of your budget on makeup if you can't see it? Lighting is a huge subject, but, with what I have outlined here, you should be able to light just about any scene you want to shoot.

■ Equipment

Good lighting does not mean you have to spend hundreds or thousands of dollars on Omni Lights and soft boxes. A trip to your local home improvement store will score you just what you need at a fraction of the price.

Aluminum clip lamps When combined with "natural light" bulbs, clip lamps will serve to light your film on a shoestring budget. Clip lamps are available in multiple sizes—I have them ranging from 4 to 12 inches (10 to 30 centimeters) in diameter. If you are concerned that you will have no place to clip the lights, you can invest in an inexpensive microphone stand with a boom attachment. The height and angle of the stand are completely adjustable, and you can clip two or three lights to one stand and then, if need be, point each one in a different direction. Microphone stands are available at any music store and are a good investment for the low-budget filmmaker. You'll wind up using them later as booms when recording audio.

Halogen work lights Besides being extremely bright, these have the added benefit of coming with their own stands to make positioning a breeze. A dual-head halogen light will cast 1,000 watts or more, depending on the type, wherever you need it. These rugged halogen lights are ideal for lighting outside and at night or for lighting large, dark areas. The only problems with halogen lights is how hot they get and the huge amount of power being pulled through the extension cords. If you have more than two or three lights plugged into the same cord, you risk tripping the surge protector or throwing the breaker wherever you are plugged in. You can burn yourself badly on a halogen light, so be careful.

01 / You can take the wire cage off of the halogen lights if it seems to be casting shadows on the scene. Just remember that the lights are hot enough to set things on fire, and those cages are there for safety reasons.

02 / Aluminum clip lamps are versatile and comparatively cheap, making them perfect for making low-budget movies.

Diffusers and bounce cards You can build a cheap, all-in-one diffuser and "bounce card" by following the instructions opposite.

Foil-backed insulation tiles also make excellent bounce cards. They typically come in sections that are about 2-feet (60-centimeters) wide by 4-feet (1¼-meters) long, can be cut to any size or shape, and are great for getting into tight spots.

You can get different effects by using different materials in conjunction with your homemade hardware. Use a colored sheet on the PVC frame to wash the scene in color. You can achieve other subtle effects by taping a sheet of colored poster board to your foil-backed insulation reflector.

Build Your Own Diffuser and Bounce Card

Step 1: Build a square or rectangular frame using PVC pipes and angle joints—they should fit together easily without the need for tools.

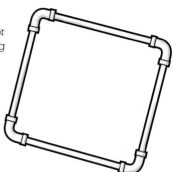

Step 2: Stretch a white bedsheet over it. Cut the sheet to fit, and sew a channel through which you can slip the PVC frame pieces. Alternatively, cut the material to the requisite size and gaffertape it to the frame.

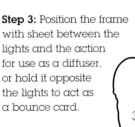

Step 3: Position the frame with sheet between the lights and the action for use as a diffuser, or hold it opposite the lights to act as a bounce card.

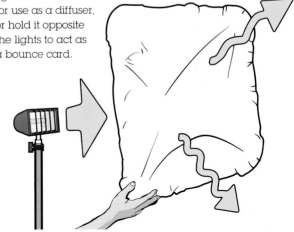

01 / If you shop around, you can find fairly cheap lighting kits. Umbrella reflectors are useful if you can afford them.

Control Box

It's possible to build a control box for your lights. A plywood box can be fit with a bunch of light switches, dimmer switches, and grounded outlets. The home improvement store will have a selection of books on DIY electrical wiring. You can plug your clip lamps into the outlets and control the intensity of each light with the dimmer switches. The more switch/outlet pairs you have, the more flexibility you'll have in your lighting setups; the more you experiment, the more ways you'll find to use your home-built equipment.

■ Lighting a Scene

Now that you have your lights and lighting accessories, we can talk about actually lighting the scene. I am only going to cover two different lighting concepts: three-point lighting and four-point lighting. In a three-point lighting arrangement, you will need a key light, a fill light, and a backlight (see opposite). Four-point lighting simply adds a background light to the three-point arrangement.

Different moods and effects can be achieved by altering the height, intensity, angle, or color of any of these lights, or even not using some of them at all. If the situation calls for it, you can use a bounce card instead of a fill light, or you can just use a key light to elicit a hard, dramatic feel to the scene. Again, experiment with it.

Often, a three-point lighting setup will cause shadows to be cast on the background elements of the frame. This is why you would opt for a four-point lighting setup. However, the background light can be tricky to place. You want to eliminate the shadows, but you also need to make sure that the light is not in the frame. This takes time and practice, and it will be a different procedure every time you switch to a new location.

Just make sure you clear a lot of time in the schedule to set up your lighting. It may take a few tries to find a configuration that works.

Three- and Four-Point Lighting Setups

Backlight This is placed behind the main subject. The backlight serves to add contours and detail to the subject as well as separate it from the background. Often you will hear the backlight referred to as a shoulder light or hair light.

Object

Background light (Four-point setup only) This is positioned so that it points at the background elements, eliminating shadows.

Fill light The fill light is placed at an angle roughly opposite to the key light, but it also lights the subject from the front. The fill light will serve to "soften" the key light and brighten any of the shadowed areas created by the key light.

Key light This is the most prominent light in the scene. The key light directly illuminates the main subject in the frame. Usually, the position of the key light will determine where you place the other light sources.

Recording sound

Besides lighting, there are few things that will make your low-budget movie seem more low-budget than bad sound. Even if everything else in the sequence is perfect, muddy dialogue can ruin it completely. If you are watching the scene and you can hear what is going on in the background better than you can hear the focus of the action, it can take you completely out of the moment.

■ On-Camera Microphones

It is distracting when the sound quality suddenly changes just because the camera angle changes. This is especially evident in dialogue scenes. The sound will be clear and crisp when the camera is focused on actor A, but as soon as the camera switches to actor B, the sound quality is completely different, and you can hear an air conditioner or some other white noise that wasn't there before. And, as soon as the camera goes back to actor A, the noise is gone.

All of these happen when the filmmaker uses the on-camera microphone to capture the audio. On-camera microphones may also pick up the sounds that the camera itself makes, because cameras that use DV tapes have motors moving the tape. Zooming in and out may cause a slight mechanical buzz. Even the sound of the camera operator pressing a button or turning a focus ring might get picked up by the built-in camera microphone.

When the camera is pointed in one direction, it can't hear what is behind it. The on-camera

01 / It is always best to use external microphones. If you don't have any, you can use your camera's microphone, but just be aware of the noisemakers in the background.

mics will pick up the sound based on the dynamics of the space at which it is pointed. Even noise in the background, which in real time may be barely discernable, will come through loud and clear on the audio track. When the camera angle changes, the microphone will pick up the completely different dynamics of the new space in front of it.

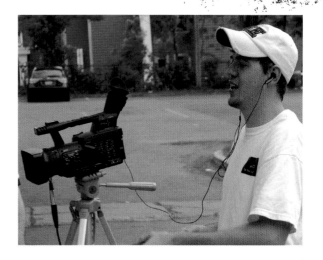

I do not mean to say that built-in camera mics don't have their uses. The omnidirectional tendencies of the on-camera mic are perfect for getting ambient room sounds, crowd noise, or nature's sounds. The on-camera mics are perfect for capturing the sounds of the undead horde shuffling their way toward the hapless villagers. Any kind of background noise that can later be placed under the dialogue tracks during editing can be captured with the on-camera mics.

■ External Microphones

External microphones can stay stationary while the camera moves to get the shot. Many consumer-class digital video cameras have audio input jacks that enable you to directly connect an external microphone for this exact purpose. External microphones also tend to be more unidirectional than their on-camera counterparts. This means that the area the microphone "hears" can be much more controlled.

Microphones can be inexpensive if you look for lower-end models. I have gotten microphones for as little as fifteen dollars, though unidirectional shotgun mics—the ideal microphone for recording movie sound—tend to be much more expensive. Cables will likely cost more than the microphone, but often you'll be able to find bundles online or at your local music supply store. If you are lucky, you can find a bundle that includes a microphone stand.

Microphone stands are an excellent investment for the independent filmmaker. Economy model microphone stands make excellent booms. A boom will allow you to get the microphone exactly where you need it while keeping the guy that is holding it well out of the shot. One thing you need to make sure you do is wrap the cable around the boom and tape it into place. Also, tape the microphone securely into the microphone clip. Otherwise, the microphone will pick up the sound of the cable pulling on the mic, as well as the sound of the entire assembly creaking in the microphone clip.

■ Boom Microphones

When recording sound, the "boom operator" should be wearing headphones and listening to the scene. In my opinion, a live ear is better than just watching the audio levels on the camera display. Headphones will give the truest representation of the sound being recorded.

01 / Microphones like this one are cheap, sturdy, and reliable.

The most difficult thing about using a boom microphone is keeping it out of the shot. Even big-budget Hollywood movies occasionally have the boom or its shadow drop into the frame.

When setting up the shot, take a second to look into the camera's viewfinder or on the monitor. Have the sound person put the mic where he or she thinks it needs to be, then get the actors to talk or, better yet, read their lines. Through the headphones, the sound person should be able

Recording Audio on a Separate Device

If your camera does not have a place to plug in a microphone, you can use a personal recorder or an mp3 player that has an audio recording feature. Digital audio recorders are relatively cheap and easily available.

If you do record audio on a separate device, be sure to use a clapboard and have someone read aloud the scene number and take number. A clapboard is indispensable when it comes to syncing up the audio to the video. Syncing up the audio and video is as simple as aligning the "clap" of the clapboard closing from the audio track to the second that the clapboard is completely closed on the video. You can keep your takes straight because the camera will see the scene and take number written on the board, and the audio track will contain someone's voice reading the same.

02 / A boom mic made from a microphone stand with a boom attachment and a cheap microphone.

03 / If you look closely, you can see the shadow of the boom on the ground. It is almost "touching" the actor. The shot was framed to exclude the ground and the shadow.

Production

to find the best placement. Now you just need to make sure that it is completely out of the frame—take a look to make sure there are no shadows thrown across the actors or on the background.

It may be difficult and it may take a little time, but you will be able to find a spot to put the mic that will be the best of both worlds. However, keep in mind that every time you change scenes or locations, that sweet spot for the microphone will probably be different.

04 / This boom is just a microphone stand with the base removed. The microphone, cable, and wind baffle came with the stand, all for around fifty dollars from a local music store. Bundles like this are common at online retailers.

■ Lavalier Microphones

If you can afford them, lavalier mics can be an asset. Lavalier mics are small microphones that clip onto, and can be hidden by, the actor's wardrobe. Typically, a lavalier mic will run to a small wireless transmitter that can also be hidden under the actor's wardrobe. The wireless receiver will connect to the camera's external mic port or input on the digital recorder in exactly the same way as a standard microphone would. However, wireless microphones are highly susceptible to interference and noise from two-way radios, nursery monitors, and the like. Also, lavalier microphones will pick up the sound of an actor moving or shifting position as his or her clothes brush against it.

Wireless transmitter

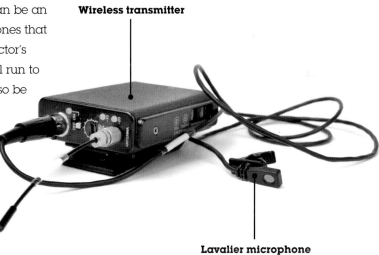

Lavalier microphone

05 / Clip the transmitter to your belt and the mic to your undershirt. Just remember that you are wearing it—you don't want to be making fun of the director while he listens in on a pair of headphones from the other side of the set.

cinematography

Choosing your shots and framing them can be tricky. Every scene is different, every movie is different, and every location is different. The frame for an action sequence is completely unlike the framing for a dialogue scene. You will need to decide how the shot will be framed based on your own preference and the aesthetic you are striving to capture. However, there are a few guidelines that can help.

Aspect Ratio

There are some basic things you'll need to keep in mind.

- If you start filming in standard definition in a 4:3 aspect ratio, keep filming that way. If you start filming the movie in high definition at 16:9, then don't switch halfway through.

- Try your best to maintain a consistent style throughout the movie—unless, of course, your story demands a change in shooting style.

- However, no movie that hopes to be distributed should be filmed 4:3. The industry standard is 16:9, and distributors will typically ignore any movie that is not filmed in that ratio. This is becoming truer every day, as widescreen and HD televisions become even more popular.

■ Focus

You'll have to keep an eye on focus. Manual focus is they way to go if you have an experienced camera operator. Quick manual adjustments will keep fast-moving action sharp and clear. Keeping things in focus manually takes a lot of practice, however, and it requires strict attention to the video on the monitor or the camera's viewfinder. Manual focus can require constant adjustment. I would opt for manual focus any time I had to shoot a close-up scene.

Automatic focus is infinitely easier, which is useful if you don't have an experienced DP. You just turn the camera on, point it where it needs to be, and film away. However, automatic focus does have its drawbacks. Often, the automatic focus feature may not be fast enough to adjust for rapid movement and action. I have seen instances when automatic focus became "confused" between foreground and background objects. The focus would spontaneously switch to something other than the action when the camera moved. I have also seen instances where automatic focus had trouble shooting through a window or through certain objects such as a chain-link fence. The camera decided to focus on the fence rather than the action happening behind it.

CASE STUDY: **RULE OF THIRDS**

In this image, the two protagonists are positioned at one of the hypothetical rule of thirds intersections. The sidewalk practically follows the path of one of the lines. This is an excellent image that would not have the same impact if the characters were placed in the center of the frame.

Here, the dead bus driver is positioned on one of the hypothetical intersections. The bus itself, as well as the pool of blood, is positioned on one line, and the ground is positioned on another. It makes for a much more interesting image than if everything were crowded into the middle of the frame.

It is a matter of preference and experience with the camera. Typically, we'll switch between manual and automatic focus depending on the needs of the shot.

■ Composition

There are a few basic rules of shot composition, which are meant to interest the viewer visually as well as maintain continuity and convention.

Rule of thirds The rule of thirds is an important one. Basically, imagine if the image in the viewfinder or on the monitor was divided into three equal sections horizontally and three equal sections vertically, as if you'd overlaid a tic-tac-toe board on top of the image. Some cameras even have a setting that will actually put this grid on the viewfinder for you. The rule of thirds states that your composition will be more interesting and engaging if you arrange things to lie along those "lines," so that the most important part of the shot should sit at one of the four intersections.

Now that you have an idea of what the rule of thirds actually is, go watch just about any movie or dramatic television series. You will see it in use everywhere.

Lead room The concept of lead room goes hand-in-hand with the rule of thirds. Lead room means that, when a moving object begins the shot on the "left line," make sure the object stays on the "left line" as the camera follows it. You should give the object some room to move into. The viewer is probably going to be more interested in where the zombie is going, instead of where the zombie is coming from.

The fourth wall Try to avoid setting up the shot so that the actors wind up looking directly into the camera; this could have the effect of breaking the fourth wall. You almost never see an actor looking directly at the camera; he or she is almost always focused somewhere between his or her face and the edge of the frame. The actor should be looking at the other actors and not the viewer. In some instances, however, you'll want to let the zombie look directly at the camera. This can have the effect of putting the audience in the place of the helpless victim as the hordes of the dead close in so that they feel a bit of the character's fear.

The 180 rule This states that objects in the frame should keep their same left/right relationship throughout the scene. If a car is racing to the right, and in the next cut it is racing to the left, it may give the viewer the impression that it has changed direction. Draw an imaginary line through the object in the frame. You should always keep the camera on the 180-degree side of that line. Breaking the 180 rule can wreak havoc in the continuity of a scene.

01 / Make sure your actors respect the fourth wall. Unless it is intended for the sake of the story, make sure they never deliver their lines directly to the camera.

■ Framing the Subject

How you frame your subject is a matter of taste, but as a general rule it is best to mix it up—use close-ups, mid shots, and long shots. The framing and shot choices that you choose will come down to your personal style and preference for each scene.

Close-ups are a good way to show what a character is feeling. A close-up will better show the facial expressions and reactions when something dramatic or traumatic happens. A good rule of thumb for a close-up is to get tight on the person's head, but include a little of their shoulders in the frame. Just the head can seem awkward, and the posture of the shoulders can help to sell the emotion.

Extreme close-ups (ECUs) are a different matter altogether. An ECU is almost solely used for dramatic effect. An extreme close-up of the actor's eyes darting to one side when he hears the zombie in the hallway is a great shot.

02 / A close-up is perfect for capturing an actor's expression when they spot the zombie.

Mid shots are shot from a medium distance—maybe getting the actor in frame from the waist up. It is close enough that you can still see subtle nuances and expressions, but you still get an idea of what is going on around him or her.

Two-shots are essentially mid shots, only you have two people in the frame.

Long shots show the actor's entire body and part of his or her surroundings.

Establishing shots are long shots with a particular focus on emphasizing to the audience where the action is taking place or what is going on around the characters.

Zooming Don't zoom. If you want to get closer to the action, dolly closer. If you want to back away, dolly back. If you don't have a dolly, handhold the camera and walk to where you need to be, or get a wheelchair if the surface is smooth. Zooming in or out will create a little bit of optical distortion and just feels unnatural.

Point of view shots The camera becomes the eyes of your subject. John Carpenter used this technique a lot in his Halloween franchise, when it seemed like you were looking out from behind Michael's mask.

Over the shoulder shots A way of filming two actors which is often used to show conversations.

directing

Directing is the most important job on a movie set. At the end of the day, it is the director's fault if something goes wrong, and it is the director's fault if the movie winds up not being any good. Every director will come at a project from a different perspective, and there are many directing "styles." Learning how to prepare, how to behave on set, and how to deal with your actors will be a big help.

■ Types of Directors

In my opinion, if you boil it down, there are two types of directors that are at opposite ends of the spectrum. First, there is the control freak. This is

01 / Frank Darabont telling his crew working on *The Walking Dead* how the shot should go.

the director who will not vary from the script. Every detail has to be perfect. The control freak will keep doing take after take after take of the same scene until you shoot something that he or she likes. This type of director will have a tendency to lose his or her temper at any minor inconvenience and will want to use a megaphone at an indoor location, just to make sure he or she has the loudest voice in the room.

Then there is the collaborator. The collaborator will take input from the cast and crew and will always be on the lookout for a better way to do something. This type of director is always willing to take a suggestion and to go with someone else's idea over his or her own. The collaborator runs the risk of letting the cast and crew take control of his or her own project.

The best director will take a little from column A and a little from column B. A good director will know when to take suggestions, but also when to follow his or her instinct and original intention for the film. A good director will be able to maintain control while not being a dictator.

■ Preparation

Whatever kind of director you are going to be, there are a few things you should do the night before or the morning of the shoot. Always review the script and the shot list. You should go over the shot list with the DP and AD and talk about how you want things framed and the angles you'd like to get for each of the scenes. Going over the shot list with the crew will keep things fresh in your mind and give your team a good idea of what you are looking for. Even if you never use the shot list at all, you'll at least have made one, and you'll already have an idea of how the scene should go when it comes time to shoot it.

If you don't know exactly what is going on for the day, the rest of the cast and crew will be able to tell you are unprepared, and they'll be like sharks smelling blood in the water. Always meet with the production team and the makeup crew before you get down to business. Get the crew all on the same page first. Once instructions and a plan of action have been given to the crew, have a meeting with the actors. Let the actors know what they will be doing, go over the pages with them, and do any last-minute rehearsals while the crew is setting up.

■ On Set

A good director needs to learn the personalities of the actors and crew. You will need to approach everyone differently. Some actors may be total method actors, while other actors may not be actors at all and need some extra direction. Some of the crew will be able to take a little bit

Stay in Control

If someone on your cast or crew is causing a problem and disrupting the set, pull that person aside and tell that person that he or she is creating issues. Never just yell and never do it publicly. You don't want to embarrass the crew member, and you don't want to come off as a tyrant.

Publicly berating the crew person will not make him or her want to work harder for you, nor will he or she be eager to change his or her behavior. Yelling at the crew person may even cause someone to walk off the set, making you both look petty and unprofessional.

If the crewperson continues being disruptive, pull that person aside again and let him or her know that his or her services are no longer required.

of instruction and run with it to do what needs to be done, whereas others will need constant supervision or else they will hang out, telling off-color jokes instead of doing their jobs. The director can't be everyone's buddy. Independent films are notorious for this. On a no-budget movie, everyone working together is already likely to be friends, and everyone will want to have fun making the movie, but a line needs to be drawn. "Goofing off" has to stop the second productivity slows. Get back to the business at hand.

Sometimes an actor will try to usurp control of your set. He'll start telling the other actors what to do, he'll start telling your DP how to frame the shots, or he will even try telling you how to direct

your own movie. Occasionally that actor may have a good idea, but just as often he will have no idea of the larger picture and how the movie will come together in editing. Pull him aside and let him know that he is the actor and you are the director. The script has been written and the shot list has been made. If he continues to try to walk

all over you and your set, make it clear that you can easily write him out of the script. Zombies have been known to eat people, and there is another actor who would only be too happy to take his place in the plot.

Like I said, if you want to make a good movie, you can't always be everyone's buddy.

01 / Whether you're making a big-budget Hollywood movie or a low-budget film, the director still needs to learn about and adapt to his or her cast and crew's personalities for production to run smoothly.

01 / If the scene isn't working, make the decision to skip it. Meet with the production team after the day's done and talk about ways to rework the scene.

■ Time Management

Sometimes a scene just won't work, no matter how many takes you get or how many different ways you try to set it up. If something obviously isn't working and won't work, move on. Don't waste time on it. After the day is done, meet with the production team and see if there is anything that can be done or rewritten in order to salvage the scene. If you think it can be rescued, try to schedule it for another day or get it when it comes time for reshoots. If it isn't going to work, forget it. A badly conceived or poorly executed scene can detract from the quality of the movie.

As the director, you have to make sure the cast and crew of your movie know there is no such thing as down time. Make it clear to the actors that if they are not needed for a scene, they should be thinking about what they need to do next. If there was no time to rehearse during preproduction, the few minutes that the crew spends getting the lighting and cameras set up is the perfect opportunity.

This lack of down time is the same for you. When you are eating lunch, you should be dumping footage or charging the camera. You should be adjusting the schedule as necessary. Eat with the AD and DP, and discuss the plan of attack for the rest of the day.

And one more piece of advice: Do not allow alcohol on your set. Someone is bound to have one too many, and time dealing with drunken crew is time you could have spent getting the next scene shot. If an actor has had too much, you may as well just pack it in for the day.

Every Shot Counts

One of the worst things you can do as a director is be unenthused about a scene. You need to be every bit as excited about the next dialogue scene as you are about the next big action scene or effects gag. Dialogue scenes and exposition are not just filler. The stuff that happens between each zombie attack is just as important to the movie as the zombie attacks themselves. You need to be excited about each and every frame you are going to shoot.

02 / It's unlikely that the cast of *Zombie Strippers* (2008) needed to be made aware by the director that there would be some nudity.

■ Working with Actors

As the director, it is your responsibility to know the story, characters, and script inside and out. If you don't know a character's motivation, you can be sure that the actor won't know it either. If an actor is unsure of the part, you need to be able to discuss how you feel the character would behave. Don't tell the actor exactly how to deliver his or her lines. Let the actor act. If the delivery is not what you are looking for, let the actor know. Tell the actor what kind of emotion you want; tell him or her what the character is feeling. Tell the actor the objective of the scene, and let the actor figure out the way to deliver the performance.

A good director should know that it will take a while for the actors to warm up. Don't worry if the performance isn't there on the first take. It may even help the performance if you give the actor some liberty with the script. If he or she can take the line and try to put it in his or her own words, you'll probably get a better performance. However, the liberties taken with the script should not affect the outcome of the story or the general plot. Ad-libbing dialogue should be the exception and not the rule. It is the actor's responsibility to know his or her lines.

Something you should never do as a director is coerce an actor into doing something they do not want to do. If your actor told you at the beginning that he or she would not do a nude scene, don't press the issue when it gets to the point in the story where you think it needs one. If the nude scene was that vital, you should have cast an actor in the roll that would have been comfortable with nudity at the outset.

Thinking Ahead

Date: 1 December

SHOT LOG Outhouse of the Living Dead				Good/Bad	Comments
				B	Flubbed line
Scene #	Take #	Time stamp	Description	G	Good take, maybe sound issue
47	1	01:43:12	Dan in the alley	G	Perfect take
47	2	01:44:35	Dan in the alley	B	Dan fell down
47	3	01:47:18	Dan in the alley	B	Zombie fell down and laughed
47a	1	01:50:22	Dan in alley, reverse angle	G	Good take
47a	2	01:52:23	Dan in alley, reverse angle		
47a	3	01:54:50	Dan in alley, reverse angle		

01 / A well kept shot log will be the editor's best friend.

One thing you should always do is use the clapboard. Put a reliable PA in charge of it, or make continuity one of the crew positions in the very beginning. One person should be responsible for keeping track of the scene and take number. Make sure they update it on the clapboard and read the numbers aloud prior to each take. This person should also keep a shot log. A shot log is a simple document that has a few vital pieces of information on it. It contains the scene number, take, time stamp, a short description of the scene, a column for good or bad, and a place for a quick comment.

You, as the director, will tell the continuity person if you felt the take was good, and then the DP will tell him or her the current time code on the camera. This will make things infinitely easier later on when you begin editing.

Always make sure you get some B-roll footage and cut-away shots. You want to make sure you have plenty of transition shots that you can insert between cuts. These can be as simple as reverse angles or a quick close-up on the actor's face. Because these are not scripted scenes, add a letter suffix to the scene number on the clapboard and when noting it on the log. B-roll can really be anything. An insert shot of some clouds, a shot of a dog gnawing on a bloody leg bone, or a random shot of some zombies walking around aimlessly all make excellent B-roll.

Throughout the entire process, you should be constantly thinking about how the movie will cut together in editing. Take a second to think of what you will need to connect one scene to the next. Every time you call "cut," you will need to figure a way to smoothly transition to a new scene.

■ There Is a Plan B

Finally, as the director, you should always have a plan B. Murphy and his damnable laws will show up at exactly the worst possible time.

In your schedule, you will have the day planned to film fifty zombies chasing the townsfolk off the end of a pier into the water. However, the weather report on that day tells you that there is a ninety percent chance that there will be the worst thunderstorm in the last 150 years. Time for plan B. Never just waste the day.

Make contingency plans. Have a rain date set up for any scene that depends on the weather cooperating. Maybe your actor will get typhus or some other exotic disease. Go through the schedule to see what can be filmed around the infected actor. If your location falls through at the last minute, have a backup. Always find something you can get "in the can." When you are done filming on that day, you can spend the next twelve hours until shooting starts again reworking the schedule.

02 / Have a backup plan. If something unpredictable happens—bad weather, someone calling in sick, a previously booked location no longer being available—be prepared to rework your script or shoot another scene.

shooting on Location

When you are making your zombie movie, you are going to need a place to stick all the zombies. You are going to need a place to put the cameras, and somewhere for the whole crew to go to the bathroom. In short, you will need to go "on location." At a most basic level, there are two kinds of locations: interiors and exteriors. Both have their own advantages and disadvanatges.

■ Interiors

Pros Filming indoors has a plenty of advantages over filming outside. When filming inside, you will typically have some amenities that are not normally available outside. Indoors, you will usually have readily available power. Never underestimate the joy of having a place to plug in when you really need it. You won't need to worry about the sound of a noisy portable generator either. Interior sets will also often have running water and bathrooms; just make sure you secure permission from the property owner before you start using them.

Interiors have the benefit of being shielded from the elements. It could be monsoon season outside, but some creative editing can make the viewer think you are in the middle of a desert. Inside sets will offer a place to stay warm when it is cold, a place to stay dry when it is raining, and, if you are lucky, a place to stay cool and air-conditioned in the hot summer. As long as you aren't shooting out a window, no one needs to know what is happening outside.

It is pretty easy to consistently light an indoor scene—if you use the same lights and put them in the same place, you will be able to duplicate a scene any time of day, any time of year.

If you get permission to do so, you can leave an indoor scene set up overnight or until the scene is finished. You don't have to worry about setting it back up the next day and possibly putting the severed head in the wrong spot. Leaving things exactly where they are is the best way to make sure you don't have any continuity mishaps in your final movie.

Interior locations have the benefit of allowing you to film in relative privacy. Depending on the location, you'll be able to "get away" with a lot more behind closed doors than you would be able to do in a public park. When you are inside, you can limit the number of people milling around the set. You probably won't have to worry about passersby wondering what is going on. You won't have to worry about the neighbor firing up his lawn mower during a take. However, setting up scenes inside does have some drawbacks.

01 / Filming indoors will protect you from most of the noise and traffic passing by on the street outside.

Cons When you are inside you will have limited space for the cast and crew to set up. With cameras and lights and makeup gags, you will often find it to be cramped. Besides needing to find room for the crew and equipment, you have to leave room for the actors to act and for the zombies to try to eat them.

When shooting inside, you have to be constantly aware of where all of your equipment is so you don't accidentally shoot one of the lights or catch an extension cord in the frame. You'll probably need to move the lights around often to chase out shadows every time you change the aspect of the camera. You need to keep in mind where all of the windows and mirrors are. We have had to do reshoots many

Note

Goo has a tendency to stain the walls, ceilings, floors, curtains, the dog, etc. I warned one director that the blood was going to come out of the goo cannon at a roughly 45-degree angle from the nozzle in every direction, and it was going to spray pretty far. He told me not to worry about it and prep the gag anyway. I am pretty sure that, even two years later, there is still blood on that stucco ceiling and in the space where the baseboard molding meets the linoleum. However, at least I warned him.

times after the director noticed that he caught a reflection of himself in the chrome napkin dispenser at the restaurant location, or he caught the reflection of a light in the glass of his actor's mother's china cabinet when she let us use her living room.

When you are filming inside, you have to be very careful about the makeup effects and the blood gags that you use. If you are going to trigger a blood gag inside, make sure you cover everything in the blast area. If your zombies are going to be oozing neat stuff all over the place, put a tarp down first. You'll have to do some creative problem solving to keep the protective coverings out of the shot, but it'll keep the location from being permanently stained.

01 / If you're shooting indoors in a place of business, be very careful with fake blood and blood gags. Your actors won't mind a bit of staining, but the manager of the store won't be quite so happy.

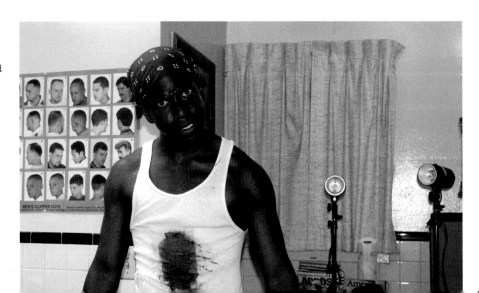

■ Exteriors

Pros There are some definite benefits to shooting outside. Outdoors you have an abundance of room. Cast and crew won't be tripping over lights and equipment, and if the PAs are in the way, you can tell them to go wait in the car. Outside, you can stage much larger shots. You will be hard-pressed to fit fifty zombies in a bathroom, as funny as that might be. Fifty zombies on a football field is no big deal.

Outside, you can be a bit more liberal with the goo. Sure, the sidewalk might have a neat bloodstain on it for a while, but it will be gone with the first rain. If you happen to get some spare brain matter on the lawn, you don't have to worry. Mow once and it will be gone.

Cons Exteriors are just that—exterior. You are out in the open. Believe it or not, people running around with realistic weapons while being chased by zombies will draw some attention.

You have to deal with environmental and possibly traffic noise. On one of the movies we've done, the production manager—who was also an actor in the movie and in full makeup/costume— had to run across a small park and ask the driver of the ice cream truck to turn off the song so we could get the take.

When you are at an outside location, there may not be power available. You may need to ask the neighbors if you can plug in an extension cord, or you may need to go get a generator, though generators are loud and very expensive. I have a relatively inexpensive power inverter that connects to the battery in my truck. This gives me two grounded outlets to use anywhere that I need them. It is plenty of power to run a camera charger and a light, or a compressor and a smoke machine. Unless you only plan to film in

Natural Light

There is no better light than natural daylight when filming. It will give you the truest representation of color and some of the most vivid images you will get. Your undead aren't vampires, remember; they won't care if it is bright and the sun is shining.

02 / Here, it didn't matter that we got blood on the ground. The field was overgrown and it was raining.

the daylight, and you only plan to film as long as one camera battery will last you, you are going to need power.

Another problem with filming outside is unpredictable weather. Rain and wind can ruin an entire day. Even if you can figure out a way to shoot in the rain, you will need to protect the camera and lights and also have a place for the cast and crew to go to stay dry. If the wind is whipping around, you can forget about recording any usable sound. Lighting may be inconsistent from day to day. If you can only film on Saturdays, you can count on it not being as sunny or as cloud-free as it was the last time you shot. Even within one day the sun shifts, and your DP should check the light meter between each take.

Dealing with the Law

When filming outside, you are much more likely to be asked for a permit. Law enforcement is bound to take notice of you, and they are well within their rights to ask you what is going on. If you do get challenged for some credentials or a permit, cooperate and be courteous. Answer the questions and don't stretch the truth too far. If you don't have any permits, tell them you don't have any. If they ask you to leave, then pack up and go. If you didn't have money for a permit, and if you do, then you probably don't have any money for bail when you get arrested for trespassing.

■ Planning for the Makeup Team

When you film on location, particularly when making a zombie movie, you will need a spot for the makeup crew to set up. At the independent level, chances are good that you won't be able to afford an effects crew equipped with their own trailer. You will need to cut off a chunk of the location to allow the makeup people to set up. This area needs to be far enough away from the action so they can keep working during takes but also close enough that you can stay in constant contact with the rest of the production team and get actors to and from the set in minutes. We have set up in garages, barns, basements, driveways, picnic shelters, and pop-up canopies, and we have even worked from the back of my truck.

Privacy Makeup can be an uncomfortable process for the actors, and people gawking at them during the application can make that worse. The extras and the crew who happen to be there watching will typically have a tendency to ask all kinds of questions about where the effects team learned how to do what they do, or they'll want to know what some material or another is. The time that the makeup team has to spend explaining gags or chasing nosy PAs out of the makeup area is time they won't actually be doing any makeup.

Some privacy will also make the day go smoother. If there is no privacy to be had, give the makeup supervisor every right to kick anyone who is a nuisance out of the immediate area.

Setup Time

The effects crew will need plenty of time to set up. There have been times that I have gotten to the set and had to immediately start applying the makeup gags. Every time that happened, it turned out to be a horrible day. I spend the rest of the day looking for supplies, not knowing where a tool is or what box contains the blood scab, and generally not having what I need, where I need it. Worse than that, I never get a chance to drink my coffee. Allowing the FX people ample time to get organized can only make the day go smoother.

Fresh water The FX crew will need some kind of fresh water supply. Keeping the crew and actors hydrated is important. Clean water is important for making bloods or thinning liquid makeup, and you need to clean your hands and tools between makeup applications. If there is not a faucet nearby, make sure that you bring several gallons of water with you to the set. Fill a few plastic milk jugs, or get a collapsible water container from a camping supply store. I've got an insulated water cooler that holds five gallons.

Power The makeup team will probably need every bit as much electricity as the DP and sound person. Wherever you have them set up, make sure there is an outlet nearby. They will need to

01 / If you're setting up a makeup studio on location, you will need to bring your own power and water.

plug in some lights to make sure they can see what they are doing. If there are any blood gags, they may need to plug in an air compressor. I usually keep an electric blender on hand as well if I need to mix up some blood or slime unexpectedly. An electric fan to keep the air moving will help in multiple ways: not only will it keep everyone cool, it will keep fumes out of the actors' faces and will help speed up the drying process on some makeup applications.

PA The effects team should have a dedicated PA while on location. It is inevitable that there will need to be a grocery store run, or they'll need coffee to keep them from passing out from exhaustion. Often they will need a supply or tool that is still in the truck. Having a PA available to do the running will save tons of time and will let the makeup crew stay on task.

Garbage The effects team will create a lot of trash. Make sure your PA ensures there are garbage cans or bags on hand to stay on top of it.

CASE STUDY: **PLACES OF BUSINESS**

We have been lucky in gaining access to some fantastic locations. We once used a local bar, and the owner was willing to give us free rein to do whatever we needed to do—as long as we scheduled the shoots for the three days of the week the bar was normally closed. With a few extras and some fake alcohol, the bar looked like it was open.

■ Etiquette

Whatever location you choose, you need to make sure you keep the owner, manager, or whoever is in charge of the location happy. I don't mean you need to bring flowers and buy chocolates; I mean that you have to treat the property with respect. Treat the location like it's your own mother's house.

If you are filming at someone's place of business, make sure you are not disrupting the day-to-day operations. If at all possible, schedule filming for a time outside the normal business hours. If you cannot get into a place of business after hours, you have to be as unobtrusive as possible. Don't have your actors screaming at the top of their lungs if you are filming in an office. Avoid blood gags and extreme effects if you film in a grocery store—whoever gave you permission may lose his or her job if the district manager sees there are blood stains all over the carpets.

Make sure that you leave the location in the same—or even better—condition as you found it. If you change anything around or move any furniture, make sure you put it back in its original location. If you bring anything to the set, make sure you take it away with you when you leave, and always clean up after yourself. Take all of your garbage out and don't leave food lying around. Insects and rodents will spot refuse left at a location the second you leave. We once filmed at a derelict train station. There were hardly any walls left and not a single

01 / We asked the owner of this property if we could get blood on his floor from a couple of "dead" bodies. He said yes, as long as those bodies were his sons.

intact door throughout the entire location. It was open to the elements and surrounded by overgrown fields. We made sure we were vigilant in keeping the refuse contained, and we took it away every night. We never saw a single rodent.

If the location has bathroom facilities and you have secured permission to use them, supply your own consumable supplies. Bring your own toilet paper, hand soap, and paper towels. Bring some garbage bags to collect the paper waste in the restroom. Chances are that the location is letting you shoot there for free. The least you can do is not use all of their TP.

Make sure you set expectations at the outset. Tell the person in charge of the location exactly what you will be doing. If there are going to be zombies gnawing on meat stumps, let him or her know. The manager may want to schedule the

Look After the Location

This seems obvious, but don't damage anything. As the saying goes: If you break it, you buy it. If some property damage does occur, you will have to fix it or pay for repairs or replacement. And it goes without saying that you probably won't be invited back.

preschool tour for another day. If your actor is going to be using profanity, let the manager know. He or she may want to keep the sales team off the phones during that scene. If you are going to be spraying blood all over everything, the manager may not let you shoot after all.

Respect the property and keep it the way you left it. If the person in charge of the location is left feeling like your movie was a positive experience, chances are you will be allowed to use the location again if you need it.

■ Health and Safety

Finally, there are some health and safety
concerns about filming on location.

Never let anyone wander around the location
alone. Use the "buddy system." Imagine if your
actor decided to explore the haunted house
location, but he went off by himself. Then
imagine that part of the floor caved in beneath
him. Your actor might find himself all alone with
a broken leg in a section of the location where
you never intended to shoot.

01 / The main safety issue with this scene wasn't creating
the car crash, it was keeping the extras away from the car
to prevent them from being cut by broken glass.

Never let anyone wander around without a
cell phone. If you can afford them, invest in some
two-way radios.

Have your AD conduct a risk assessment
for every location and then circulate it. All your
cast and crew need to sign it and abide by its
recommendations. Use common sense. Safety is
paramount. Your movie is not worth anyone's life.

CASE STUDY: **SHOOTING ON LOCATION**

Always clearly mark any specific hazards at any location. On one of the last movies I worked on, we neglected to do that, and it resulted in a fairly serious injury. We were at a derelict train station. For some reason, there were pits in the floor at irregular intervals. These holes were there on purpose. We have no idea why they were there; we only know that they were plenty big enough for an entire person to disappear into one of them. It was approaching dusk, and there were no lights in the building other than what we brought. We were between takes, and an actor had to visit the outhouse. The pit in the floor was not marked or cordoned off with any kind of high-visibility tape. The actor did not see the hole and literally stepped into it. She fell nearly 6 feet (2 meters) down onto jagged rusted metal, chunks of broken concrete, splintered pieces of wood, and who knows what else that wound up in that hole after thirty years of abandonment. It took three of us to get her out of that pit. She was bloody and in shock, and we had to carry her from the building to an area where emergency services could get to her. She is fine now, but things could have been tragically worse if she were alone.

The whole thing could have been avoided if we had thought ahead and marked the hazard. Even if we just sent someone with her who had a flashlight, she may have seen the hole. It is easy to look back now and say that we should have done something different. We never thought anything like that could happen, but once it did, it seemed like what we should have done to prevent it was just common sense.

02 / If going off on your own can't be avoided, make sure a few people know where you went.

A Happy crew

A happy crew is a productive crew, and it is not hard to keep your cast and crew content. If it's your movie, it is also your responsibility to make sure everyone is well-fed, properly hydrated, comfortable, and working within their limits. If your set is running smoothly, you will get much better results.

■ Scheduling Is a Courtesy

First, manage the call times. If you know the actor won't be needed until noon, don't make him get to the set at 8 A.M. If you know an actor is going to need to be in makeup for three hours, plan that accordingly. Don't make the actor get there early to get into makeup and still expect him or her to act for twelve hours. Likewise, don't make the

effects department get to the set at 7 A.M. to start applying the gags when you still plan to be shooting bodies and zombies at 9 P.M. Keep in mind that when the shooting day ends, it will still take the actors an hour to get out of makeup. It'll take another couple of hours for the makeup crew to prep for the next day. Your twelve-hour day can easily become a fifteen-hour day or more for some of the crew.

Always try to plan for a ten-hour shooting day, because ten hours can easily turn into twelve if you get a couple of problem scenes. Try to avoid shooting for more than twelve hours. Your cast and crew will start to lose focus and concentration around the ten-hour mark, though a good director should be able to squeeze those two extra productive hours out of them. Any more than twelve hours and your cast and crew will start to get cranky. Also, try to ensure that there are at least twelve hours between the end of one shooting day and the first call for the next.

01 he first ones to get makeup will also be the first ones to get ﹍﹍nky because of the wait for their scenes.

■ Catering

Always make sure you feed the cast and crew. Seriously, feeding everyone helps you to get your movie made. A big portion of your budget will to go toward food and beverages. Keep bottles of water available all day and try to keep something on hand for your people to snack on. You don't need to bring out the wine and cheese, but at the very least you should keep a bag of pretzels or even some donuts around. If your crew is hungry, they will likely spend more time focused on their stomachs than on the next scene. Make sure everyone stays hydrated as well. Dehydration is a productivity killer.

At about the halfway point of your shooting day, make an actual meal available to the cast and crew. It does not have to be anything fancy. We have had all kinds of meals while on set. The best idea is to mix it up and try to do something a bit different every day. Order pizzas on one day and get sandwiches on another. We have found that bringing a grill to the set is a cost-effective way of feeding everyone a hot meal. I have never been on a set where hot dogs and hamburgers were not a hit. Always make sure you find out if any of your crew has any specific dietary needs. Have some tofu or veggie burgers available for the vegetarians. If you have a diabetic, make sure you have something low-carb and sugarless.

I would not recommend trying to feed tons of extras. Schedule your day so that the extras can be wrapped and gone before lunch, or don' schedule them to come in until the meal is done.

02 / Feeding the crew often means that they have to grab a slice of pizza on the fly because there is a crisis that needs to be dealt with before shooting can start again.

It sounds shady, but it will save you time and hundreds of dollars in the long run.

Bring a coffee pot. Caffeine is a lifesaver on a movie set, and brewing coffee yourself is infinitely cheaper than getting it from a coffee shop.

■ Safety and Comfort

Bathrooms Considering that you are feeding everybody and making sure they stay hydrated, you will also need to make sure that there are facilities nearby for them to use. If there are no bathrooms available on the set, you may need to scout around for a restaurant or some other place close to the set that has a public restroom. Check in and make sure they won't mind if your crew stops in to use the facilities from time to time. If you can afford it, you can rent an outhouse, but they can be pricy—especially if you are only filming on the weekends. Renting a porta-potty does not make sense unless you will be filming for a number of days straight at the same location.

We filmed at a small house that had been abandoned for several years. There was no running water at the location; hence, there were no toilets. The director made arrangements ahead of time with a retail store that was only a few minutes away.

First aid Always bring a first-aid kit. Keep an assortment of adhesive bandages on hand, antiseptic ointment, alcohol wipes, aspirin, aspirin-free painkillers, bug spray, burn ointment, and cold packs. Make sure you keep the first-aid kit in a central location and appoint someone on set who knows how to use it all. Make sure everyone knows where the first-aid kit is located. I am very accident prone, so I also keep a cane and a set of crutches in my truck at all times. If someone gets a cut or a scrape, handle it right there and move on. If someone gets seriously

hurt, get them to a hospital. Use some common sense, though. There is no need to call 911 for a broken arm, but if someone is bleeding profusely from the face and head, you may want to call for an ambulance.

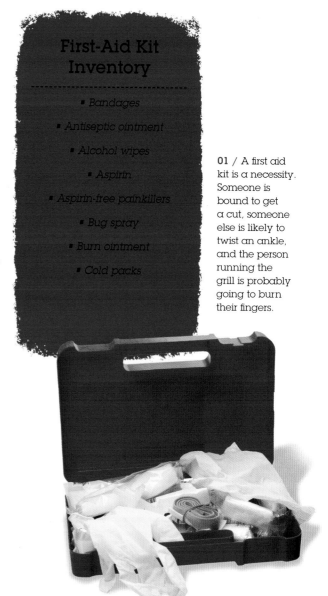

First-Aid Kit Inventory

- Bandages
- Antiseptic ointment
- Alcohol wipes
- Aspirin
- Aspirin-free painkillers
- Bug spray
- Burn ointment
- Cold packs

01 / A first aid kit is a necessity. Someone is bound to get a cut, someone else is likely to twist an ankle, and the person running the grill is probably going to burn their fingers.

■ Down Time

Finally, give the cast and crew a place to take a break if they need one that offers some kind of protection from the elements. Bring some folding chairs so they don't have to sit on the ground and some blankets so they can lie down on the ground. If it is raining, make sure there is somewhere that everyone can stay dry. If it is cold and snowy, provide a place for them to stay warm. Do your best to keep the cast and crew comfortable, even if you have to let some of your actors sit in your car with the air conditioner on.

Basically, you should treat the whole cast and crew as you would want to be treated.

02 / Making a movie requires people to work long days. This actor had been on location before dawn broke, so we let him get in a quick nap rather than rehearse his lines again, since it would be another hour before we needed him.

postproduction

Postproduction is going to be nearly as exhausting as preproduction. It is when you will take all of the footage and cobble it into a cinematic story. You'll add sound effects, re-record dialog, add some visual effects, and decide if you need to do any reshoots.

This is when you'll find out if everything you did in preproduction, your efforts as a director, the skill of your DP, and the performance of your actors paid off. It's also when you will learn to despise the phrase "fix it in post," and you'll develop a deep, seething hatred for every person who has ever or will ever utter those words.

Postproduction will always take longer than production and just as long as preproduction. The director and the editor will be spending a lot of time together for the next few months. The producers and any investors will want to see some samples and screen captures from the movie as it begins to come together.

No matter how much you might want to, do not rush postproduction. Take more time than you need to ensure that you end up with a movie you can be proud of. I have worked with directors who have announced premier screenings before principal photography was even completed. Don't do it. Don't give yourself a deadline to have the movie finished—if you get ahead of things, you will find yourself more concerned with getting the movie finished to meet a self-imposed deadline than getting it finished with the attention to detail that it deserves.

I have worked with directors who tried to schedule postproduction to be completed in time for submission to festivals. Don't do this either. If you want to get the film into a festival, but the deadline is sooner than you'd like, wait until next year to enter it into the competition.

Spend more time polishing your movie than you need to. Show your rough cut to an audience and get some feedback. Don't take negative comments as a personal attack. Be willing to take suggestions and re-edit scenes. I have worked with directors who go through the trouble of setting up test screenings only to ignore every suggestion. Sometimes your scene just will not work as you've edited it. Admit that it can be better, and redo it.

Editing

Editing can be a long and tedious process, but it is the editing that will tell your story. Modern editing software is a dream that was unknown to editors only ten years ago. Digital video and nonlinear editing suites make the job easier. The more vigilant you were during production in keeping shot logs, the easier the editing will be.

■ Preparing for the Edit

Editing involves watching the same chunk of footage over and over again and the same shot a hundred times from a dozen different angles. You have to pick the best takes from the best angles and splice them together, somehow making the transition from shot to shot feel seamless.

Transfer your footage You have to dump all of your footage every day, but you shouldn't just copy the files and move on. You need to organize the files as you go. Every camera is different, however, and will handle recording and dumping footage differently. Read the camera manual and make sure you are dumping the footage in its raw, uncompressed state. Every time you compress or change file format, you can potentially lower the quality of the video.

Be organized Make a top-level folder for the entire project. If you are using DV tape, create a folder labeled with the tape number. If you are using some type of media card, and you have

Rule Number One: Save Often

Save on your computer, save on an external drive, save your raw project files to DVD. The only time you shouldn't save your progress is when you are willing to lose all of that progress. External hard drives are getting larger in capacity and smaller in price every day. Blank DVD-Rs are dirt cheap. Online data storage is becoming more and more common. Save your files in multiple places.

if you don't save often, you may lose your work, or worse, lose the original files altogether. One of the movies I worked on is gone forever except for the sub-par edit that still exists on DVD. The director had all of the raw files on his computer, and only on his computer. One catastrophic crash later, everything was gone. We wanted to go back and re-edit it to try to make it a better movie, but now that is no longer possible.

01 / The DP is using a digital video camera. Once the tape is full, he'll number and date it. The shot log will have a corresponding number which makes it easy to know where a specific bit of footage is.

the resources to use a different card every day, create a folder labeled with the card number. Obviously, you can skip this step if you have to constantly reuse the same media card or you are filming with an HDD camera.

Next, create a subfolder labeled with the date you shot the footage. Within that folder create subfolders for each scene number. In each scene folder, you'll need to keep a logical folder structure and stick with it. Refer back to the shot log when it comes time to organize the clips into individual folders.

Rule Number Two: Save Often

Really. I can't drive this point home enough. Save your files often and in multiple locations. It will have taken you a good bit of time to dump and organize the footage. If you are using an HDD or reusing a media card, this is especially important. When you wipe the drive or card when prepping for the next shooting day, the only place the footage will exist is wherever you just saved it.

■ Software

There are numerous software editing suites on the market. Usually, you will get a basic editing application bundled with your camera. The major operating systems typically come standard with basic video editing programs as well. Microsoft Windows includes Windows Movie Maker, and Mac OS comes with iMovie. There are also open source—which are also free—video editors for Windows, Mac, and Linux. All of these "free" applications will get the job done. Prosumer applications such as Apple's Final Cut Pro and Adobe Premiere have utilities and features that will make the job easier, but they come with a big price tag.

What these editing packages all have in common is that they are based around a timeline. The concept is relatively simple. You import your video and sound files to the application and then just drag them to where you want them on the timeline. There is a whole lot more to editing than that, but that is the basic principle.

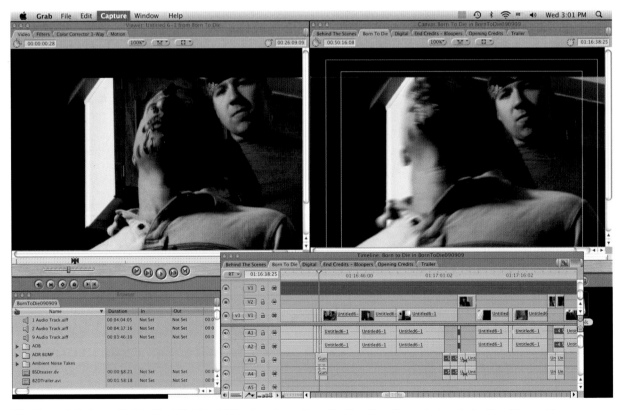

01 / A movie being edited in Final Cut Pro. Notice the elements on the time line: Items designated with a V are video snippets while items designated with an A are audio.

■ The Editing Process

Take notes From your shot log (see page 108), you will already know which are the best takes. Watch the rest of the takes again anyway. You may find something that can be salvaged and used in the scene when you intercut it with some of the B-roll and transition shots. Keep a notebook handy, or a blank shot log, so you can take notes while you are rewatching all of the footage.

Pay attention Watch the performances carefully. Close your eyes and listen to the dialogue. Study the body language and reactions of the other actors. Listen to the quality of the sound, listening for lawn mowers, dogs barking, or cell phones ringing. Pay attention to the focus. Watch again to make sure there are no boom mics or unwanted reflections in the frame.

Experiment Cut a few different versions of each scene. Once you start putting things together a different way, you may find that the second or third version of the scene is better than the first.

Take your time Each page of script translates to roughly one minute of screen time. Each minute of video on screen will take approximately one hour to edit. Adding and syncing audio and sound effects will also take approximately one hour. Color correcting and grading will, again, take approximately one hour. Do the math: For each minute of your movie, you can expect to spend at least three hours in editing.

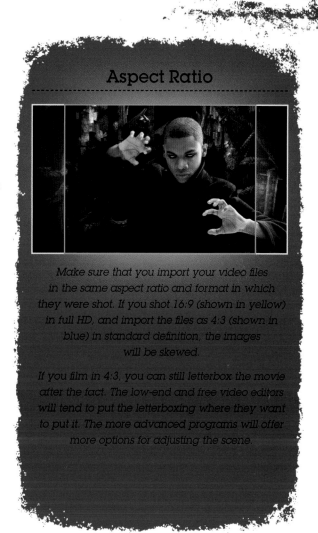

Aspect Ratio

Make sure that you import your video files in the same aspect ratio and format in which they were shot. If you shot 16:9 (shown in yellow) in full HD, and import the files as 4:3 (shown in blue) in standard definition, the images will be skewed.

If you film in 4:3, you can still letterbox the movie after the fact. The low-end and free video editors will tend to put the letterboxing where they want to put it. The more advanced programs will offer more options for adjusting the scene.

Rule Number Three: Save Often

The only time you shouldn't save is if you are willing to lose all the work you have done.

■ Rules and Guidelines

There are a few basic editing principles and practices that you should know. Then you can break the "rules" as you see fit.

Don't jump around Let the viewer know where the scene is taking place at the beginning or the end of the sequence—don't put an establishing shot in the middle of the scene. If you are halfway through a dialogue scene, shot in a relatively close-up frame, don't suddenly cut to a wide shot of the building in which the scene is taking place and then jump back to the close-up frame.

Dialogue When editing a dialogue scene, make sure you have some overlap in the conversation. Don't wait until the actor has completed his portion of dialogue before switching angles. Cut to the other actor before the line is complete, that way there will be no unnatural pauses.

Reaction shots A zombie getting hit in the face with a sledge hammer is sure to elicit a response from the survivors witnessing it, so cut to those reactions. Reaction shots and close-ups also make excellent transitions from one take to the next.

Rule Number Four: Save Often

You will have never used as much profanity as you will when the power goes out while editing a particularly complex scene.

01 / This scene was a struggle between this girl and an escaped convict. Most of the scene was shot wide, except for the close up of her face during the fight. Her reaction to the struggle helps to sell the scene.

Be consistent If the camera is in motion in one take, make sure it is still in motion in the same direction in the next. If you start the scene using takes that were shot handheld, stay handheld throughout the scene.

Be flexible Nonlinear editing and digital files mean that you never have to be stuck with a bad edit. You can go in and change a scene as many times as you need to get it right. You can cut twenty different versions of the same scene while never altering the original source material.

Always be willing to lose a scene if it just won't work. Sometimes there is no way to cut the takes together so that they work to get the idea across. Even if you spent several days shooting the scene and spent tons of money on effects and makeup gags, you should be willing to lose it if it isn't good. If it is a bad edit, it is a bad edit and should be cut from the movie.

■ Reshoots

Sometimes you may find that you need to reshoot a scene altogether. Maybe the focus was bad in the take, maybe a setting on the camera was wrong, or maybe you need to shoot a new scene that was never written in the original script. If a pivotal scene needs to be included so the movie makes sense, but the takes you have are just not any good, you're going to have to bite the bullet and do some reshoots.

Reshoots involve getting permission to use a location again. You have to schedule a crew and hope that the actors you need will be available. You have to bring the same lights and camera and make sure that the location is exactly the same as it was during the initial shoot. This means you must check that the location has not been repainted if it is an interior, or they have not put a Wal-Mart up in the location if it was an exterior.

You have to make sure that there is no snow on the ground in the reshoot if the original takes were in the middle of summer. You need to keep continuity in mind regarding all of the background elements as well as the actor's wardrobe. You have to hope that the actor has not lost or gained a significant amount of weight and that he or she still has the same hair or facial hair style. You have to make sure the actors are in the same makeup, and they are

02 / Watch the reshoots on a monitor before calling it a day. A monitor or TV screen will be clearer and easier to see than the viewfinder or display on your camera.

Note

I don't think a director should ever edit his own movie. He is too close to the material. Asking the director to cut a scene from his film is akin to asking him to cut off one of his own fingers. If a director is in love with a take, he will do anything to keep it in the movie—even if it means that it will take away from the quality of the finished movie.

running away from the same zombies. The effects crew must be able to reproduce the same gag or appliance for the reshoots, provided they still have enough supplies to accomplish what you need.

Finally, make sure you watch the new footage on a monitor before you are done. The last thing you need to happen is have your camera on the wrong setting or the action still out of focus. This has happened to us. We have needed to do re-reshoots.

adding audio, visual effects, and credits

Audio, music, visual effects, titles, and credits should not be just an afterthought— they are an integral part of your movie. Crisp-sounding dialogue, well-designed graphics, and thoughtfully selected music can make all the difference to the final result. And remember—never, ever leave anyone out of the credits.

■ Sound Effects and Audio

When it comes time to sync up your audio, there are several tools you will have at your disposal to make it easier. If you used the clapboard (see page 108) while filming, syncing external audio is a simple task. The clapboard consists of two basic parts. One part is a chalk board or dry erase board, where the scene/take information of the upcoming scene is written. This board is then connected via a hinge to a clapper. The clapboard will have a series of diagonal lines on both halves that match up perfectly when closed.

All you need to do is to sync the snap sound, or clap, on the audio track to the exact second that the board is closed and the diagonal lines are perfectly aligned on the video. You will know that your audio track and video match because someone will read aloud the information on the clapboard, and you will be able to see the scene and take number written on the board.

01 / ADR—just a fancy term for recording the dialogue over again because what you originally captured is not usable.

Rule Number Five: Save Often

You won't be happy when the cat walks across the keyboard, accidentally deleting the new audio files.

Replacing dialogue If you have to re-record dialogue, or do ADR (automated dialogue replacement), syncing up the new dialogue to sit exactly where the unusable dialogue exists is also a relatively simple concept. When the soundtrack is sitting on the timeline in your editing program, you will be able to see it represented by a wave form. A character's delivery of dialogue will have a unique shape on the timeline. When you bring the new dialogue onto the timeline, you just match up the new wave form to the old.

Use the same microphone and recording device that you used to record the original sound. Different microphones will record with different tonal qualities, and different recording devices tend to add their own character to the sound. It will be obvious on the final edit if you place audio with totally different characteristics into the scene.

ADR is not easy. The actor has to put himself in the same frame of mind and get back into character—maybe months later. You have to get the actor to deliver the line with the same cadence and rhythm as he did the first time.

Sound effects Adding sound effects is as easy as dragging them onto the timeline. However, adjusting the levels and timing may take some practice to get them to fit naturally in the scene. Take your time when syncing the sound effects. The sound of a punch that is not synced perfectly to the action, even if it is only off by a few milliseconds, can take a person completely out of the scene and destroy the illusion.

02 / The same dialogue, delivered by the same actor, with the emphasis on the same syllables, will produce a new waveform that is almost identical to the original.

Foley

Sometimes you will have to record some foley. Foley is sound effects you record on your own, such as footsteps or the sound of the zombie dragging its feet across the sidewalk. You may want to record the sound of chewing and ripping and bones crunching. Record the sound of breaking some celery and carrot sticks. Record the sound of squishing raw meat in your hands. Capture some growls and groans. You can overlay all of these recorded sounds on the timeline, even combining the sounds to get some custom homemade sound effects.

■ Music

No movie is complete without some kind of score and music. The soundtrack contains the songs that might play in the movie. The score is the music that plays in the background and is typically instrumental. You need music. It is as important as sound effects and clean dialogue.

You should never "steal" music, or put a song in your movie just because you like it. Often, you will need permission from the label that released the piece, as well as the artist who performed it.

If you know any people who play in bands, ask them if they would be interested in recording some original music for the soundtrack. Ask these same musicians if they would like to help you with the score. You don't need a full orchestra to score your movie. You only need a couple of musicians to watch your movie and play what it makes them feel.

You can also search for royalty-free music or songs that have passed into the public domain. Public domain simply means that the copyright has expired, or there was an open license to begin with, and you can use it as you see fit.

Rule Number Six: Save Often

Your visual effects person may actually be legally allowed to kill you if you lose the work he or she spent countless hours creating.

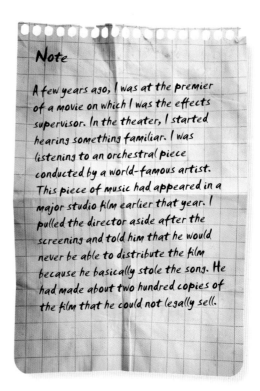

Note

A few years ago, I was at the premier of a movie on which I was the effects supervisor. In the theater, I started hearing something familiar. I was listening to an orchestral piece conducted by a world-famous artist. This piece of music had appeared in a major studio film earlier that year. I pulled the director aside after the screening and told him that he would never be able to distribute the film because he basically stole the song. He had made about two hundred copies of the film that he could not legally sell.

■ Visual Effects

Sometimes you may want to add a visual effect, or a scene may require some digital magic to play the way you intended. You will need a visual effect for any scene that is either beyond the reach of your budget or just not possible for you to pull off. If the city is supposed to be in flames, I am fairly certain that the mayor might have a problem with you walking around town with loads of matches. When the zombie's head bursts open after you hit it with that ten-pound sledgehammer, you may decide that there needs to be just a bit more goo splattering all over. Digital effects work best, in my opinion, when you marry the computer-manipulated elements with live, practical footage.

01 / If the director wants to frame the shot so there is no way to hide the blood rig, you'll need to add digital blood.

Accomplishing digital effects is a complex and time-consuming process that requires the skill of a person who knows exactly what he or she is doing. The software required for digital effects is a pricey investment too. As a new filmmaker with a limited budget, I would highly suggest doing as much as you can on set.

If you know that a scene will require some visual effects in post, work out the angles and shots in advance with the visual effects artist. Try to have the artist on set when you are shooting that scene to make sure that you get the shot you want, and the artist gets the elements he or she needs to accomplish the effect in post.

Color Correction and Grading

Your first foray into the realm of digital visual effects could be simple color correction and grading. Color correction basically means that you are making sure that the black color is the same black from scene to scene, the whites are the same, and so on. You can go a step further and apply a color "wash" to selected scenes or to the entire film. Adding warm and cold tints to the picture can elicit different subtle emotional responses from the viewer.

You can spend a year at an art school, and you will have still only scratched the surface of color theory. So, my suggestion is to play with the settings. Toy with the color and see what you like. Just remember, if you don't like the color grading that you apply, click one button or change one setting and you have removed it.

■ Titles and Credits

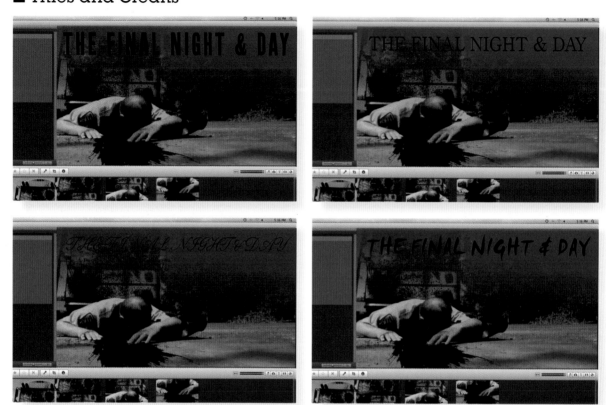

01 / While you can use any font style, size, or color that you want for your titles, the text needs to be legible. The script font used on the lower left is almost unreadable in this context.

Editors tend to create the titles and the end credits as the final stage of postproduction. The titles are the names of the production company, the director and writer, the names of the lead actors, and even the title of the movie. The titles are all the words that fly by at the beginning of the movie. The end credits are a complete list of all of the actors and everyone who worked on the movie, everyone who helped with the movie, and all of the extras. The most important thing about titles and end credits is to make sure you spell everybody's name correctly. Use the signed contracts and releases that you collected at the beginning of production to make sure you have all the names right. Also, meet with the production team and make absolutely sure you aren't forgetting to thank someone or give credit when it is due. Slighting someone in the credits, even if it is completely unintentional, can guarantee that the missed person will never help out again.

■ After the Edit

Once the movie is edited to your satisfaction, you'll have a sample-quality version that you will be able to watch within the editing application. You won't get a high-quality, DVD-worthy version until you render the movie. Rendering the film is when you will choose the final format of the film, what the movie will play on, what kind of compression will be involved, and so on.

Rendering takes a long time. Start rendering the movie and go to bed. Then get up the next morning and go to work. Then come home and watch your favorite television program. Then you should check on the rendering process. Seriously. Rendering takes a long time, especially on a home computer that was not specifically designed for editing video. Assuming you rendered the movie for DVD, you can now burn the rendered files to a DVD.

The moment of truth has arrived. You now have to watch the DVD to check the final version of your zombie movie.

If you notice any jagged edges or if the video seems to skip or play rough, chances are that the video file was not deinterlaced correctly in the rendering or DVD authoring process. The software and hardware combination you will use makes it impossible to tell you exactly the right method to get the best-quality DVD. You will, once again, need to refer back to the manuals and the Internet. It may take you a few tries to get the movie rendered and burned to a quality that you like.

Television and DVD Standards

NTSC is the standard TV format in the United States, Canada, and Japan. PAL is the standard in Europe and the UK. There are six DVD regions including region 1 (United States and Canada), region 2 (most of Europe), and region 4 (Mexico, Central and South America, and Oceania). There is also an unofficial "worldwide" region 0. Burn the movie for the region where it will be released.

02 / Rendering a movie takes time. A lot of time. Don't sit around waiting for it to finish; leave your computer running and go do something else.

getting your movie seen

Now that you have your movie "in the can," you just need to do something with it. You have to get your movie out there and get it seen. You have to do some promotions, marketing, and, ideally, make some sales. The Internet has made this much easier in recent years, but you should still leave your bedroom once in a while to promote your work. Been there, made the movie, printed the T-shirt.

You have spent a lot of your own time and money. Your friends have donated a lot of their time to you and sacrificed the last dozen Saturdays to your movie. You've all devoted a great deal of resources to telling your story. You want people to see the movie, but I am pretty sure that you don't want them all to come to your house to watch it.

So, you'll need to schedule a screening for the cast and crew. In fact, you should think about scheduling a couple of screenings.

However, before screening the movie, you need to do some promotion and develop some marketing materials. Make some movie posters or something cool to hang in the theater that will make people want to see the film. Posters and other gimmicks will help you sell tickets. Promotion will help you sell the movie. This is why you absolutely need a trailer.

Wrangle some reviews of your movie and put the good ones on the DVD cover. You need to start thinking about film festivals and conventions. Festivals are a great way to get recognition. You'll have to think about ways to distribute the movie, whether it will be on DVD, Blu-ray, some kind of video on demand, or for a digital player such as an iPod. More than likely, you will have to self-distribute the movie, but there is that lucky one-in-a-million movie that will get picked up by an established distributor. One in a million. Those odds aren't so bad.

01 / *Colin* (2008) is an enjoyable film which, it was claimed, only cost seventy dollars to make. With that sort of budget, any distribution—even self-distribution—will make a profit.

02 / A good poster can be all it takes to make someone want to see your movie. Just don't give everything away on the poster; the trick is to give them just enough so that they want to come in and see more.

marketing

You will need to do some marketing and promotional work. You don't need to employ a big public relations company; you just need to do some legwork on your own. Start by making a trailer that shows off the highlights of your movie.

By now, you should already have a couple of versions of the investor kit that I suggested you make back during preproduction. One version will be the investor kit for investors, while the other version will be the one you used while trying to secure locations and get permission to shoot your movie. You need to make a third version that will be your media/PR kit. The beauty of this is that you are pretty much using the same document over and over—you just need to change a couple of words here and there and add some pictures and production stills to it. You will include this media kit with every copy of the movie that you will eventually send to festivals, reviewers, and, if you are lucky, distributors.

■ The Trailer

Editing trailers is an art form in itself that takes some practice. Watch some trailers online, especially for zombie movies that you have already seen. Pay attention to the pacing and edit points in the trailer. You want to get viewers interested and leave them wanting to know what will happen next. Paint a very broad picture of the plot, but not enough to give anything away.

01 / Make sure you put some good stuff in the trailer, but not the best stuff—leave the viewer wanting more.

For a zombie movie, you'll probably want to stay away from lengthy dialogue scenes—though a particularly strong line delivered by a good actor can't hurt.

Music is also important to the success of a trailer. You can use the songs you already have for the movie, but you may want to score the trailer in the same way you did the movie. Quick cuts and frenetic editing are generally the way to go for a zombie movie. Long, steady shots, slow dialogue, and no dramatic music can kill any sense of tension in the trailer and leave the viewer thinking that the movie will be boring.

■ Other Visual Tools

Go through all of the production stills that you should have been grabbing since day one. Go through the movie and take screen captures. Get some great shots of some of the images that you feel represent the movie, and use them in your marketing materials.

Poster design A good poster is important, so take some time creating it. Talk to the editor or the person who did your visual effects. It is more than likely that one of them will have access to some kind of image-editing application and a desktop publishing suite. If not, there are some open-source programs available that can do almost anything the pricy ones can do. An Internet search on "open-source image editor" and "open-source desktop publisher" will return a few options that will work on just about any operating system.

You really should put the title of your movie on the poster. If you made another Batman movie, just the bat symbol on a black background might be enough. However, if you just made *Outhouse of the Living Dead*, no one will have any idea what the lone blood spattered porta-potty is all about.

Use an interesting font. Arial or Times New Roman are not what I would call interesting. Look online—there are some excellent fonts available for free, and some excellent font packages available that are pretty inexpensive. However, when I say interesting, I don't mean hard to read. You want John Q. Moviegoer to be able to read it at first glance.

Cool stuff Some other good marketing ideas are easily distributable materials such as postcards, T-shirts, and buttons. Online vendors can supply you with hundreds of screen-printed shirts for a few dollars each, which you can turn around and sell at screenings for twice what you paid for them. Postcards adorned with some slick graphics, the website, and the showtimes of any screenings can be left at bars and restaurants, especially at locations where parts of the movie were shot. More postcards, buttons, and other little gimmicks are great to give away at screenings, festivals, and conventions.

THE FINAL NIGHT & DAY

02 / T-shirts are great for publicity—just think of the number of people who you walk past each day.

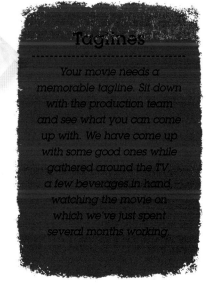

Taglines

Your movie needs a memorable tagline. Sit down with the production team and see what you can come up with. We have come up with some good ones while gathered around the TV, a few beverages in hand, watching the movie on which we've just spent several months working.

internet Marketing

The Internet is a fantastic resource for the low-budget filmmaker. Getting your own website is inexpensive, and once you're online, your movie is just an Internet search or a social networking link away from one quarter of the planet's population.

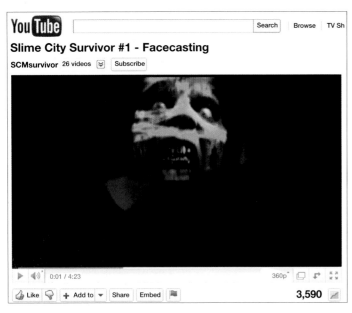

01 / On the set of *Slime City Massacre* (2010), the director had someone shooting behind-the-scenes stuff every day. A few days later, a series of YouTube videos detailing the production were posted.

■ Getting an Online Presence

Use all of the social networking sites to your advantage. Social networking is free, and damn near everyone in the moviegoing world is no more than two or three degrees of separation away from someone with a Facebook account.

Put your trailer up on son of the free video-hosting sites. Pr some behind-the-scenes video up as wei. Millions of people hit YouTube every day, and there are several other sites that get nearly that many visitors. The Internet is an odd place; you never know when the next video will go viral.

Build a website. You can find all-in-one hosting and template packages for little or no cost. If you use an all-in-one package, you can have a custom website built for your own movie in just a matter of minutes. Upload your trailer to your website, upload all kinds of pictures, including behind-the-scenes stuff. Put links to your website all over the social networking sites.

Get listed on the Internet Movie Database (IMDb; www.imdb.com). There are some hoops to jump through, and it can take a little while, but it is a great promotional tool. IMDb has some instructions on the title submission page that clearly explain what will make your movie eligible, because they will not just take anything.

■ Reviews

Scour the Internet for sites that review horror movies. Start sending emails asking about getting your movie reviewed. Many sites will be happy to review your movie, while just as many others will be happy just to take a free copy of your movie while never writing a single word about it. You have to be careful and prescreen the site on your own—read the reviews that are posted on the site already. Use some common sense. Tito's Basement Movie Reviews may be a real site, but if he doesn't have any reviews posted, you can probably be safe in skipping that one. Whoever you send a review screener to, make sure to include a stripped-down PR kit.

Getting reviewed in printed magazines would be amazing, but this is pretty hard to do.

Magazines are highly selective about what they print because of the limited space and the high cost of printing. Websites can publish as much content as they want as often as they like. Not to mention that the popular magazines might get thousands of indie filmmakers, just like us—only not as cool—sending movies in every year.

One thing you can definitely do is get some coverage in the local newspaper. The local media loves to hear about things going on in their own backyards. Local arts papers will often be willing to review the movie, give you coverage during production, and publish showtimes.

02 / The AMC television series based on Robert Kirkman's *The Walking Dead* helped raise the profile of zombies in pop culture. Take advantage of this when you market your movie.

screenings

Screenings, festivals, and conventions are good, though sometimes expensive, ways of getting your movie seen.

■ For the Cast and Crew

Minimally, you need to have a screening for all of the cast and crew. Call around to some local movie theaters, because many will be willing to rent time on their screens. As long as they have the capability to project digitally, you should have no problem. Some old theaters only have the capability to project film, so you need to check before you book the cinema. Unless you opted to shoot on film and have a 35-mm print you can bring with you, digital will be your only option.

As long as you aren't looking for a prime time slot, you should be able to get a theater relatively cheaply. We have gotten a three-hundred-seat theater on a Thursday evening for just about three hundred dollars. However, a good weekend spot can cost two or three times as much. Let's say that you do book a three-hundred-seat theater. Even if you were to give away one hundred tickets to cast, crew, and their guests, you would still have two hundred tickets to sell for four or five dollars each. That will pay for the theater and then some.

When you are selling tickets, it is a safe bet that the cast and crew will be able to sell some to their families and friends. The managers or

01 / Wherever you have a screening, have copies of the film available or some kind of merchandise relating to the movie on hand to sell to the public.

owners of the locations at which you filmed might be able to sell some tickets. Definitely leave some tickets at the venue. If you get some coverage in the local media, you will almost always get walk-ins wanting to buy tickets.

■ Festivals and Conventions

Film festivals will typically charge a submission fee, and you will enter your movie in one or more categories. Paying the fee does not guarantee acceptance, so be prepared to lose your fee. Many will want you to send some kind of press kit with the movie. Luckily, you already have one.

There are horror film festivals all over the world, and some accept submissions internationally. Join some festival submission websites such as withoutabox.com and shortfilmdepot.com. Withoutabox festivals generally require a fee, but Short Film Depot features festivals outside the United States that offer free submission. Check out *MovieMaker* magazine's annual "25 Festivals Worth the Fee" list—they usually profile at least a couple of horror-specific festivals.

Film festivals are excellent exposure if your movie gets accepted. However, one of the best things about your movie being selected for a film festival is that you can put "Official Selection of Whatever Film Festival" on the cover of the DVD. Even better, if you win in any of the competitive categories, you can put that on the DVD cover as well. Film festival selection and awards can only help you eventually find distribution.

Some film festivals will even allow you to set up a table to hawk your wares. This is the ideal place to bring out those postcards, buttons, or whatever other little gimmicks you have devised for the movie. Bring a supply of DVDs to sell as well.

Besides festivals, go to the horror and sci-fi conventions. Vendor tables at these shows are available to anyone who can pay the fee.

Big conventions get an incredible amount of foot traffic, and people who go to these shows go with the intent to buy stuff. A lot of people will plan their month around conventions and save up a good bit of disposable income. The problem is that there are hundreds of other vendors just like you hoping to get the convention attendees' money. You need to make yourself visible. The flashier your booth or table, the better your product looks, and the more goofy stuff you give away, the more copies of the movie you'll sell.

Some of the bigger conventions show movies. Find out what you need to do to get your movie on the list. Do whatever it takes. The more visible you are, the better you will do at the conventions.

Major Horror and Fantasy Film Festivals

- Screamfest, Los Angeles, CA
- Fantastic Fest, Austin, TX
- New York City Independent Horror Film Festival, NY
- Buffalo Screams Horror Film Festival, Buffalo, NY
- Eerie Horror Film Festival, Erie, PA
- Fantasia International Film Festival, Montréal, Canada
- Sitges International Fantastic Film Festival, Spain
- FrightFest, London, UK

packaging and selling your DVD

You can get away with supplying DVD-R screeners to reviewers and sending burns out to festivals. However, when it comes to selling your DVDs, DVD-R copies look totally amateur. Even with the best DVD cover art that you can manage, a DVD that you burned yourself will detract from the presentation.

There are other problems with burning the DVDs yourself. Every now and then, you'll get a bad burn—the disk will just not play. It could have been a bad disk from the manufacturer, or more likely, a hiccup in the burning software. If you sell someone a DVD for ten dollars and it doesn't work, word will get around. At the very least, that person will never buy a product from you ever again.

01 / It looks unprofessional to sell a DVD for ten dollars or more that has the title written on it in permanent marker.

The worst thing you can do is sell a movie with the title written on the disk in permanent marker. We have been guilty of this in the past, but we didn't know any better at the time. You should avoid using the self-adhesive DVD labels that you print yourself. We tried this too, in an effort to not look as bad as we did when we wrote the title on the disk in marker. The only problem is that the printed labels can throw off the balance of the disk. If a label is even a fraction of an inch off from perfect center, the disk will wobble in the DVD player and skip, hang, or not play at all.

There are disks that are manufactured with a printable surface on the label side. These are great if you have a printer capable of printing on a disk. However, the inkjet printers that do this are pricy, and the ink cartridges cost a small fortune. Also, think of the time you will spend burning and labeling hundreds of disks. Doing it yourself, you have the benefit of making disks on demand, though you can wind up paying over three or four dollars per disk in supply costs alone.

02 / *The Pigman* cover was printed on a laser printer at a copy store and it doesn't quite fit the case. The other three movies were professionally pressed and printed.

03 / A professional duplication company can make multiple copies of your movie simultaneously, saving you time and therefore money.

■ Professional Production

The better option is to have your DVDs professionally pressed. Companies offering such a service should be able to produce your DVD, silk-screen the label art directly onto the disk, print the front and back sleeve, package the whole thing, and shrink-wrap it. The companies that provide these services will typically have a quality-control department that will check to make sure that your DVDs look and play as they should before they get shipped to you.

If you do get your DVDs manufactured professionally, keep in mind that the more you order, the less expensive it will be. It may seem to be prohibitively expensive to get it done, but do a little bit of math.

You can get five hundred professionally printed DVDs with full-color disk art and jacket in a standard DVD case for about two dollars per unit. Conversely, if you order one thousand, the cost per unit will only be a little more than a dollar.

So for five hundred disks, you'll pay about a thousand dollars. If you spend one hundred to one hundred-and-fifty dollars more, you can get the full one thousand disks. Even if you sold the movie for five dollars, you are still making a profit. If you price the disk at ten dollars and sell the lot, you can more than likely recoup expenses for duplication and a good portion of the money you spent to make the movie. You do, however, run the risk of being stuck with a thousand DVDs if no one buys any.

■ Distribution

You can try to get professional distribution for your movie. Occasionally, a distributor might buy the movie from you for a lump sum and then take care of all of the duplication and marketing themselves, but this probably won't happen unless you already have some kind of proven track record of success with your movies. More often, they won't give you a dime unless they see a substantial profit first. Every company will have their method of buying the rights to and distributing a movie; just have someone look over the contracts before you sign anything.

Some distributors will only buy movies at film markets, and it can cost ten thousand dollars or more to represent yourself or screen your movie at a film market, not to mention travel and lodging expenses. You can get a sales agent or someone to represent you at the markets, but these agents will probably have a dozen other movies that they are trying to sell at the same time, and they charge top dollar for their services.

■ Self-Distribution

Do what you can to find real distribution, but remember that there are several thousand movies made independently every year. If the big boys don't come knocking, you have to self-distribute to get your movie out there. Self-distribution is more than likely going to be the route for the small independents like us.

Very often, local media stores will have a "homegrown" section. There are even some national chain stores that will carry a selection of locally produced books, albums, and movies. These stores will usually sell your wares on consignment.

Locations that were featured in the movie will often be willing to keep a display up and a stock of your movie on hand.

Sell your movie at festivals and conventions. Team up with other local filmmakers and split the cost of having screenings, then sell your DVD at the theater.

01 / When self-distributing your film, sell it wherever and whenever you can. Every screening and every convention or festival you can afford to attend are places where you'll find potential buyers for your movie.

02 / Screamfest is a popular horror-centric film festival in Los Angeles, California. The film submission fees are very reasonable for those of us on a tight budget.

Contact any local haunted houses and see if they would be willing to promote your movie. Often they'll let you set up a table to sell DVDs near the entrance to the haunt.

Sell the movies on your website and on Internet auction sites. Always carry a couple of copies of your DVD with you everywhere you go.

Online Distribution

Services like Createspace.com, a division of Amazon, will distribute your movie "on demand" for a cut of each sale—albeit a big cut. You can try to get your movie on Netflix, but this is another process that involves a lot of waiting and several hoops that need to be jumped through.

You never know when the subject of conversation will shift to movies and the fact that you just happen to have recently made your own movie. You have to be creative.

Finally, be persistent. You have poured your heart and soul into the movie. You have spent countless hours editing scenes where your friends get mauled by legions of the undead. You have spent all of the money that you can spare on the production, and have spent even more money that you couldn't spare on printing the DVDs.

Make people want to see the movie. Talk it up like it is the greatest movie since the invention of the camera. Believe in what you are doing. Don't ever let anyone tell you to give up or that you can't make movies. If this movie doesn't sell like you hoped, or if it does not get the recognition you hoped it would, then make another movie. Just keep going. If you stumble and fall, get up again and keep on at it.

Because if you don't get up, the zombies will get you.

Glossary

ADR Automated Dialog Replacement—recording new dialogue at postproduction if the sound recorded when a scene was originally shot is not usable or a line of dialogue needs to be changed.

Appliance A false wound or other physical alteration which you will apply to an actor. In this book, the terms appliance and prosthetic are used interchangeably.

Aspect ratio The ratio of the long edge of a frame to the short edge such as 4:3 or 16:9.

B-roll footage Inserts and cutaway shots that are not scripted scenes. A quick close-up, a shot of the night sky, or even a second camera catching a different angle of a scene can be used for b-roll.

Back light Illuminates the focus of the scene from behind. Used to separate the focus from the background elements.

Background light Illuminates the background to eliminate any shadows caused by the other lights.

Blending edge Where an appliance meets the skin. Thin edges are easier to hide.

Bounce card A generally flat, somewhat reflective surface which is used to bounce light back onto the subject from one or more light sources. Often used to add fill lighting to a scene.

Breakdown sheet A page used to outline the details of an individual scene to make it easier for the crew to film it.

Climax The turning point of the story where all of the problems posed by the plot come to a head.

Close-up Filming the subject at close range. If shooting a person, a close-up would be a shot of the head and top of the shoulders.

Composition The arrangements of individual elements in the frame. The way you compose the shot will direct where the viewer's eyes go.

Conjunctivitis Commonly known as pink eye. It is an infection of the mucous membranes around the eye which can easily be caused by poor hygiene practices.

Dermawax A waxy material developed for use by morticians in order to "fix" parts of the anatomy on a dead body. Soft, flexible, and easy to sculpt, it is a temporary medium.

Diffuser Used to soften the illumination coming from a hard light source.

Dolly Moving an entire camera in a smooth motion. It also refers to the equipment that a camera is attached to that allows it to be moved in a smooth motion.

DV Digital Video—an electronic recording system which is a cheaper and more flexible alternative to recording on traditional film. Digital video eliminates the need for costly film processing fees.

Establishing shot A wide shot which is intended to show to the audience where the action is taking place.

Exposition The part of the story where background information is provided and characters are introduced.

Extreme close-up Filming the subject at very close range. If filming a person, an extreme close-up would be a shot of the just the eyes.

Extrinsic coloring Painting the outside of an appliance after it has been pulled from a mold.

Fill light Illuminates the focus of the scene from a different angle than the key light. Used to soften shadows.

Flocking Small, threadlike fibres that are suspended in the casting material when coloring an appliance. Flocking adds a dimension of depth and color to a prosthetic piece.

Foley Recording sound effects that are added during editing such as recording the sound of carrot sticks breaking to imitate the sound of bones snapping.

Foreshadowing Giving hints to what will come later in the plot.

Fourth wall The "wall" between the audience's reality and the film.

Gag For the purpose of this book, a gag refers to any of the effects that the movie will require.

Gelatin A reusable and inexpensive casting material used in making prosthetic appliances.

Glycerine Replaces some or all the water in the gelatin formula.

Goo A generic technical term for any of the slime, blood, or other nastiness you intend to slather all over your actors. I call some of my blood rigs "goo cannons."

Hydrocal A white gypsum cement which is stronger and harder than plaster of Paris, but not as hard as Ultracal-30.

Intrinsic coloring Adding pigment or flocking to a casting medium prior to pouring it into a mold so that the resulting appliance will be colored when pulled.

Investor kit An information pack which is given to potential investors. Normally an investor kit will include a synopsis of the film, some production art, marketing details, and other related material.

Isopropyl alcohol A widely used solvent and cleaning material. It is available in a variety of different strength solutions: Seventy percent is the common strength of rubbing alcohol; ninety nine percent is the strength used with alcohol-activated makeup and to clean and sterilize brushes.

Key light Directly illuminates the focus of a particular scene.

Lead room Relating to shot composition, it is the area in front of a moving object. By having more space in the direction an object is moving than behind it, the viewer gains the impression that the object has space to move into.

Long shot Filming the subject at long range to show the actor's entire body and surroundings.

Methyl cellulose A plant-based thickening agent found in many products. I use it for the base of most of the goo that I make because it isn't sticky and it doesn't draw insects like corn syrup.

Mid shot Filming the subject at medium range so that the viewer can see both the actor and what is going on in the immediate vicinity.

MSDS Material Safety Data Sheet—these contain all of the pertinent health and safety information for a particular chemical or compound.

Nitrile gloves These are far more hypoallergenic, stronger, and puncture resistant than latex gloves.

Nonlinear editing The ability offered by DV to edit footage without having to cut a film strip or manually move forward and backward through a tape.

NSP Clay Nonsulfur Polymer Clay—the absence of sulfur makes this a perfect sculpting medium when you are planning to use silicones.

Outline A way to see your ideas on paper in some kind of logical order.

Point of view shot Filming in such a way that the viewer sees the action unfold through the protagonist's eyes.

Over the shoulder shot Filming from over one actor's shoulder, normally to show him or her in conversation with another actor.

Postproduction The stage after production when the film is edited, sound and video effects and credits are added, reshoots are planned, and so on. You will also begin to market and promote your film during postproduction.

Preproduction The stage when you'll prepare for production by, for example, writing the script, generating storyboards, choosing your cast, seek permissions and permits for locations, and agree to contracts.

Production The stage at which you are actively shooting your movie.

Prosthetic *see* appliance.

Pry point An area of a sculpture or mold that allows you to pry the piece apart.

Registration key Points in each half of a mold that fit together like a puzzle to ensure your mold sections line up perfectly.

Reshoot Filming replacement or additional scenes at the postproduction stage.

Resolution The part of the story after the climax, when all of the details are wrapped up.

Rising action The part of the story that follows exposition and leads up to the climax.

Rule of thirds Relating to shot composition. The frame is divided into thirds horizontally and vertically. Focus is placed on one of the lines or an intersection between two lines.

Shot list A list of the shots you want to get on a particular day's shoot, with a brief description of framing and camera angles.

Shot log A running list of the takes for each scene with notes to record the time code, quality of performances, and whether the director thought it was a good take or not.

Side A small section of script given to the actors during auditions.

Silicone For our purposes, a two-part rubber used in making hypoallergenic prosthetic appliances.

Silicosis The result of breathing silica dust. It can lead to chronic breathing problems.

Sorbitol A material for adding strength and tear resistance to gelatin prosthetics.

Squib Something that will burst a blood gag to imitate a bullet hit.

Storyboard A visual representation of the script that shows how a scene should work before the filming starts.

Tetrodotoxin A neurotoxin obtained from puffer fish. The basis of "voodoo zombification."

Timeline Relating to editing software. The entire movie is edited around the timeline. Elements such as sound and visual effects are added to the timeline of the film.

Ultracal-30 A very hard and precise gypsum cement used in mold making.

Undercuts This is an undesired part of a life cast or sculpture that will cause the mold to lock, forcing you to start over again.

Zoom Using the camera's lens to move in or out from the action, rather than moving the entire camera closer or further away.

index

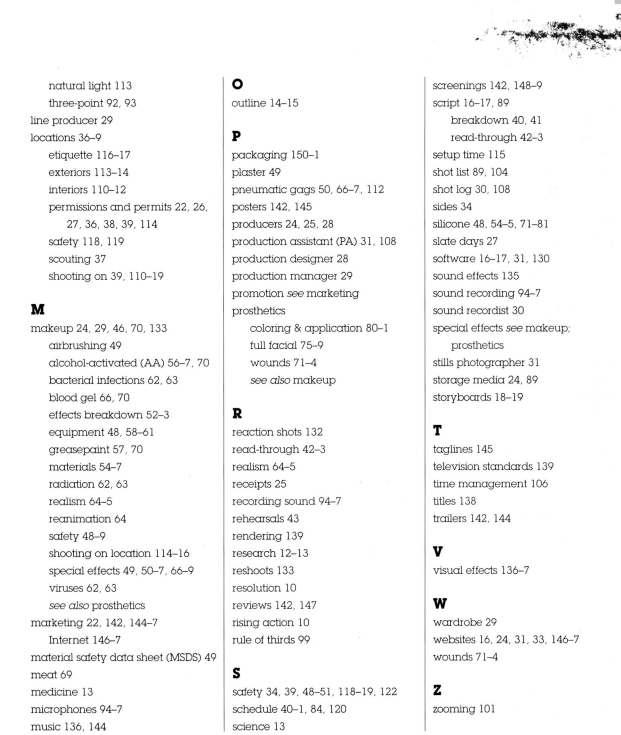

acknowledgments

The author would like to thank Greg Lamberson, Tammy Janinum, Kyle J. Kaczmarczyk, Adam Steigert, Bob Lingle, Jay Mager, Michael O'Hear, Dan Monroe, Arick Szymecki, and Phil Beith for their help in putting this book together.

The publisher would like to thank the following for permission to reproduce copyright material:

Kobal: AMC-TV: 1, 84, 102, 147; Big Talk/WT 2: 7 (top); Constantin Film/Davis-Films: 124 (foreground); Dimension Films: 127; Dimension Films/A Band Apart 14 (bottom); DNA/Figment/Fox/Peter Mountain: 12–13, 17; Fox Atomic/DNA Films/UK Film Council/Susie Allnut: 101; Image Ten: 6, 11; Lions Gate 8 (foreground); Lorimar 5; Nowhere Fast Productions: 142; Palace/Film 4/Br Screen: 44 (foreground); Pariah Films: 47, 85, 105, 140 (foreground), 143; Re-Animated Productions/Empire: 64; Renaissance Pictures: 24; RKO: 12; Scream HQ: 107, 144; United Artists 7 (bottom); Universal Studios: 20 (foreground); Variety: 2, 46, 126; Weinstein Co./Steve Wilkie: 82 (foreground); Wingnut Films: 103.

Fotolia: Creative: 3; Georg Preissl: 33 (left); Joe Gough: 36 (middle); Daryl Marquardt: 36 (bottom); Eric BVD: 36 (right); Carlos Caetano: 37 (middle); Fedor Bolba: 37 (right); Brooke Fuller: 87 (right); Winiki: 87 (bottom right); SG: 94; Luminis: 97 (bottom right); Ra3rn: 122; Paul Hakimata: 131; Inna Yurkevych: 135 (bottom right); Ekler: 137 (bottom right); 2happy: 150; Blake Sandifur: 151 (top right).

Getty Images/Michael Buckner: 153.

Deftone Pictures Studios: 99 (top left, top right), 100, 132, 137 (top), 138.

Kyle Andrews: 148, 152.

Rob Brandt: 67, 68 (top right, right, bottom right), 91 (top right, right, bottom right), 93.

Tammy Janinum: 30, 66, 116.

Kyle J. Kaczmarczyk: 18 (top), 19 (top left, top right).

Greg Kapsiak: 113.

Jason Mager: 130.

Dan Monroe: 134, 135 (top right), 139.

Michael O'Hear: 22, 57, 62, 63 (bottom), 65 (middle left, middle, middle right, far right), 68 (left), 69 (bottom right), 70, 81 (left, right), 92, 111, 115, 129, 133.

Adam R. Steigert/Christopher Brechtel/Stephanie Andrews/Kyle Andrews: 4, 18 (bottom), 19 (bottom), 23 (top), 23 (bottom), 27, 28, 29, 31, 32, 35, 38, 39, 42, 43, 49, 50, 51, 54, 58 (bottom left), 59 (bottom right), 60 (top), 61 (bottom), 63 (top), 65 (bottom left), 69 (top left), 71, 86, 88, 89, 95, 96 (bottom right), 97 (top right), 106, 109, 112, 117, 118, 119, 120, 121, 123.

Arick Szymecki: 75, 76 (top left, top right, bottom left, bottom right), 77 (top left, top right, bottom left, bottom right), 79 (right), 80.

Michelle Zurowski: 55, 58 (bottom right), 59 (middle), 60 (bottom, bottom right), 61 (top), 72 (top left, bottom left), 73 (top left, top right, bottom left, bottom right), 74 (top left, top right, bottom left, bottom right), 78 (top left, top right, bottom), 79 (top left, bottom left), 90, 91 (top left), 96 (top left, bottom left), 151 (top left).